THE SETTLEMENT
— OF THE —
AMERICAN WEST

Joan Chandler

OXFORD

Contents

Oxford University Press, Walton Street, Oxford OX2 6DP
Oxford New York Toronto
Delhi Bombay Calcutta Madras Karachi
Petaling Jaya Singapore Hong Kong Tokyo
Nairobi Dar es Salaam Cape Town
Melbourne Auckland

and associated companies in
Berlin Ibadan

Oxford is a trade mark of Oxford University Press

1 Introduction

The Background

In the year 1790, Americans did not know what the Rocky Mountains looked like; they had never heard of the Grand Canyon. Most of them lived in towns and villages in one or other of the thirteen states that made up the United States of America. And these towns and villages had been long settled, some for over 150 years. The population was mainly of British descent, Scots, Irish and Welsh, but there were Swedes, Dutch-men, and Germans too. African slaves made up about a fifth of the population.

As well as these American people who had recently fought and won their independence from Britain, there were other Europeans in North America. In the 1500s, Spaniards from the Caribbean and Mexico began to explore what is now called Arizona, New Mexico, Florida and Texas. By 1800, the Spaniards had settlements in all these places and in what is now

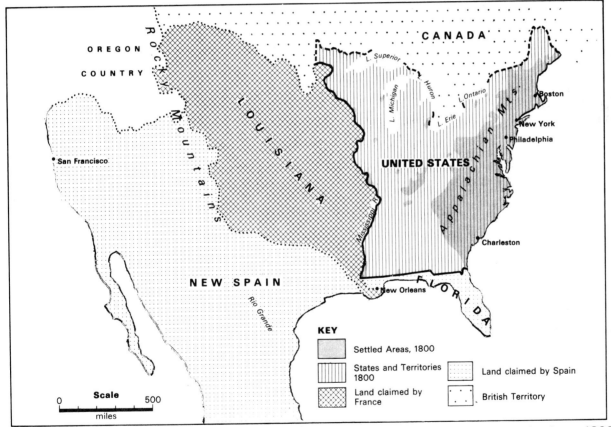

KEY

Settled Areas, 1800

States and Territories 1800

Land claimed by France

Land claimed by Spain

British Territory

This map shows the areas of North America claimed by different European countries in about 1800, and the places in the United States where people had made their homes.

California; and they had explored parts of Utah and Colorado. Spanish priests taught Christianity to the Indians, and soldiers and farmers settled and farmed the land.

There were French in North America too. In fact most of the inhabitants of Canada at that time were of French descent and had been under British rule only since 1763. The French had been the first to explore the Mississippi and Ohio rivers as well as the Valley of the St. Lawrence where so many had made their homes, and France still owned vast tracts of land.

Long before white men from Europe reached America, Indians inhabited the land. There were hundreds of different tribes; some hunted in the forests of the northeast; some depended on buffalo in the plains; some lived on the plants and animals in the arid areas of what is now Arizona and New Mexico.

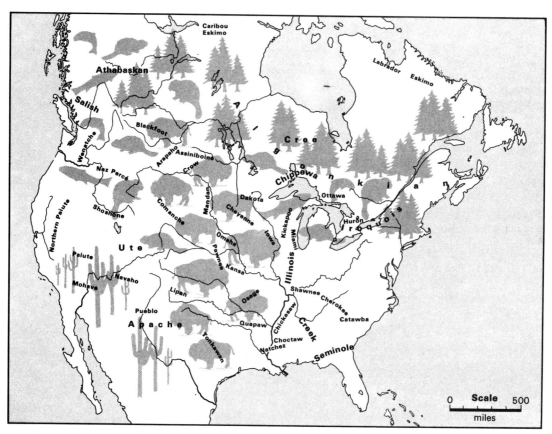

The map shows where some of the Indian tribes lived, in about 1650.

How the United States grew

The thirteen original States had to work out a way of ruling themselves as soon as they became independent of Britain. By 1787 their leaders had worked out a Constitution. Each State kept the right to rule its own local affairs; it had an elected governor and group of men who could make laws.

But there was also a central or Federal Government which dealt with important matters such as making war, fixing customs duties, coining money, which concerned all the States. The head of the Federal Government was the President, who was elected. Laws were made by the elected members of the House of Representatives and the Senate. Together they made up the Congress.

Congress had to decide how to govern the new lands of the west. After the war with Britain (1783) the U.S. owned land from the east coast to the Mississippi. The new land northwest of the River Ohio was called the Northwest Territory. Congress decided who its governor and judges should be; and said that when 5,000 free men lived in it, it could elect its own group of lawmakers. As people began to settle there the land would be divided into three, four or five States, and when 60,000 free men lived in one of these States, it could become one of the United States in its own right, and send representatives to Congress.

In 1803 President Jefferson bought a huge stretch of land from Napoleon, the Emperor of France, for 15 million dollars. The U.S. suddenly doubled in size.

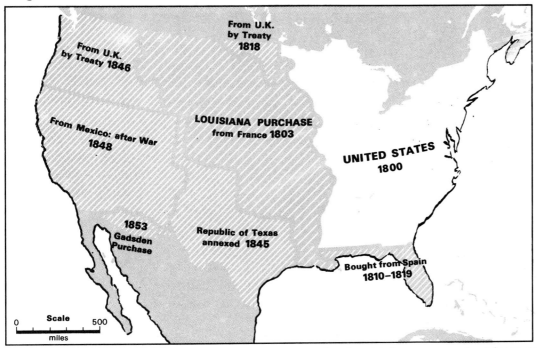

The map shows the Louisiana Purchase and other lands which were acquired later on.

Who Went West?

First just a few trappers and hunters and farmers searching for their own land travelled westwards through the Appalachian mountains; soon this tiny trickle of people became a flood, moving westwards. People went in canoes, in steamboats, on horseback, in covered wagons and on their own weary feet. They went looking for furs, for gold, for land, for freedom from religious persecution, or to save souls.

Some just went looking.   Many died on the way.

Emigrant train in Colorado

A miner's ball

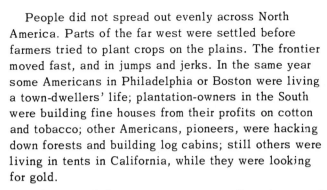

People did not spread out evenly across North America. Parts of the far west were settled before farmers tried to plant crops on the plains. The frontier moved fast, and in jumps and jerks. In the same year some Americans in Philadelphia or Boston were living a town-dwellers' life; plantation-owners in the South were building fine houses from their profits on cotton and tobacco; other Americans, pioneers, were hacking down forests and building log cabins; still others were living in tents in California, while they were looking for gold.

Make sure of the PLACE you are reading about, and of the TIME.

A rising city of the west

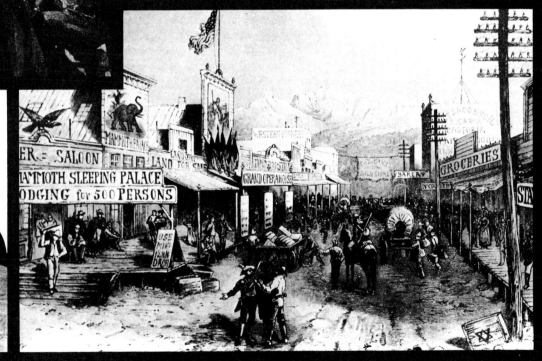

ILLUSTRATIONS BY COURTESY OF RADIO TIMES HULTON PICTURE LIBRARY

Differences between North and South

The original thirteen colonies were very different from one another.

The climate changed from the cool north to the hot south and so crops and vegetation were different. Farms in the north tended to be small, and farmers could not use many slaves. The plantation owners in the south, growing rice, tobacco and cotton, needed a great deal of unskilled help; slaves provided it. Small landowners in the south copied large ones; to own a slave or two was a sign of prestige.

As frontiersmen from the North and South went to the West, they took their two ways of life with them. Northerners used their own strength, Southerners favoured a society based on slave labour.

As new States were formed in the West, the problem of whether they should be slave or free loomed large. People could not agree; in 1854 Congress found it impossible to decide whether slavery should or should not be allowed in the new Territory of Kansas and Nebraska, so the people were left to decide for themselves. Believers both in slavery and freedom rushed to settle in Kansas; each group hoped to have larger numbers than the other.

The disagreements between the North and the South became so acute that war between the States broke out in 1861. By 1865, the North had won. Slavery was made illegal throughout all the States, so any slaves who had been taken West or who had escaped to new Territories were free.

Sources of Extracts and of Illustrations

The extracts in the booklets come from letters, diaries, verses, and books which were written by men and women who knew the people and places they wrote about.

Some of these pieces of writing were printed soon after they were written; others were stored in special collections in private or public libraries.

Historians have read these writings, and have arranged for the publication of many of the longer pieces. Historians have also used some of the shorter documents in their own modern books.

The illustrations mostly come from the same period as the extracts, except for a few modern photographs and the captions show which these are.

Some of the settlers drew sketches showing their way of life. Artists travelled in the west and drew what they saw there. George Catlin, for instance, went to the west especially to draw pictures of Indians while they still lived more or less as they had done before white men went to the U.S.

Other artists tried to recapture the spirit of life on the frontier, when it was changing very rapidly. Frederic Remington was born in 1861; and while he spent much of his time in the west he often drew pictures from his imagination instead of sketching actual scenes, as Catlin did.

Books and magazines were often illustrated by engravings. Sometimes the artists drew from their imaginations, or made the scene more spectacular than it really was, to catch the reader's eye.

Until the modern film was invented in the late nineteenth century, each photo had to be taken on a heavy plate which was exposed for several seconds.

2 The expedition of Lewis and Clark

No white man had ever travelled across the American continent from the River Missouri to the Pacific Ocean until Captain Meriwether Lewis and Captain William Clark did it. In 1803, President Thomas Jefferson asked them to lead an expedition to the Pacific.

President Jefferson had had such an expedition in mind for some time. He knew that the Missouri River flowed eastwards. He also knew that the Columbia River flowed westwards. But neither he nor anyone else knew quite where these rivers started from, nor how close to each other they were. Jefferson hoped that the distance between the rivers would be short; then a trade route could be developed right across the country, by water. Then goods from Canada could be taken across land, and through the United States, profitably, instead of being shipped round Cape Horn.

Look at the map. Which mountain range lies between the headwaters of the Missouri and the Columbia rivers? Can you tell from this map alone whether a trade route of any kind was possible?

Roughly how far did Lewis and Clark have to go, to get to the Pacific from St. Louis?

What would you need to know, before you could make an intelligent guess about how long such a journey might take?

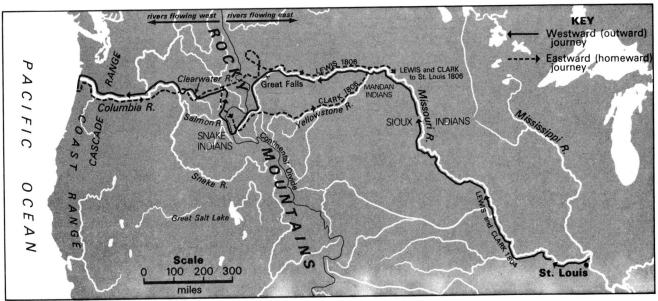

This map shows the route Lewis and Clark took from St Louis to the Pacific coast.

An American artist, Catlin, went to the West in the 1830s, to paint Indians. Catlin drew this picture of part of the Missouri river, which must have looked much the same to Lewis and Clark.

Instructions

Besides exploring the Missouri River to see whether a trade route could be developed, President Jefferson told Lewis and Clark to find out about Indians; how many there were, of what tribes; what they wore and ate; what their laws and customs were. Jefferson wrote:

treat them in the most friendly manner which their own conduct will admit; make them acquainted with the position extent, character of the U.S. of our wish to be neighborly, friendly and useful to them . . . if a few of their influential chiefs, within practicable distance, wish to visit us, arrange such a visit with them.

Lewis and Clark had to look at their surroundings as well; President Jefferson asked them to note:

the soil and face of the country
the animals of the country
the mineral productions of every kind
volcanic appearances
climate

The first part of the journey

Lewis and Clark took about 30 people with them; they spent the winter of 1803–4 organizing the trip, and training the men. In May, 1804, the party set out in a keelboat, and two other open boats, rowed by men who would be sent back to St. Louis the following spring.

The boats pulled steadily upstream, until they met the Sioux Indians, who had caused traders trouble for years. Lewis and Clark talked with them, gave them gifts and went to a feast; but the Indians hung about the boats for three days. Ordway, one of the men on the expedition, wrote about the fourth day:

Some of the chiefs were on bord insisting on our Staying until the others came. We told them we could not wait any longer. they then did not incline to let us go on . . . about 200 Indians were then on the bank. Some had fire arms. Some had Spears. Some had a kind of cutlashes, and all the rest had Bows and steel or Iron pointed arrows. then Captain Lewis ordered every man to his place ordered the Sail hoisted.

The Indians realised that if they attacked, many of them would be killed, in spite of their numbers. So they begged for a gift of tobacco instead; and then let the boats go on up the river.

This was the only time that the expedition had real trouble with Indians. Most of the time, the Indians were friendly and helpful, and Lewis and Clark relied on them for information about rivers, mountains, hunting and so on.

British Museum

This picture, drawn by Patrick Gass for the book he wrote when he got back from the journey, shows a more usual scene, where Lewis and Clark are in council with the Indians.

They went upriver until they reached a tribe of the Mandan Indians. Catlin later painted this village.

12 | THE SETTLEMENT OF THE AMERICAN WEST

The first winter

The expedition built a wooden fort to spend the winter in.

They discussed the best route with the Indians. Snow fell; ice closed the river. Clark wrote, on December 7th, 1804:

the river Closed opposit the fort last night $1\frac{1}{2}$ inches thick, The Thermometer Stood this Morning at 1 d below 0. three men frost bit badly to day.

In the spring the ice melted; by April, everything was ready for the expedition to go on. The boatmen were sent back to St. Louis with reports, letters and specimens the expedition had collected. Lewis wrote, on April 7th, 1805:

we were now about to penetrate a country at least two thousand miles in width, on which the foot of civilized man had never trodden; ... and these little vessels [6 canoes and 2 rowing boats] contained every article by which we were to expect to subsist or defend ourselves, however, enterta[in]ing as I do, the most confident hope of succeeding in a voyage which had formed a da[r]ling project of mine for the last ten years, I could but esteem this moment of my departure as among the most happy of my life.

Unknown land

Lewis and Clark attended to the President's instructions. On April 22nd, Lewis wrote:

Coal or carbonated wood pumice stone lava and other mineral appearances still continue ... I ascended to the top of the cutt bluff this morning, from whence I had a most delightful view of the country, the whole of which except the vally formed by the Missouri is void of timber or underbrush, exposing immence herds of Buffaloe, Elk, deer and Antelopes feeding in one common and boundless pasture. we saw a number of bever feeding on the bark of the trees alonge the verge of the river, several of which we shot, found them large and fat. walking on shore this evening I met with a buffaloe calf which attached itself to me and continued to follow close at my heels untill I embarked and left it.

Conditions, however, were far from ideal. On April 25th, Lewis wrote:

the water friezed on the oars this morning as the men rowed. about 10 oclock A.M. the wind began to blow so violently that we were obliged to lye too.

There were other difficulties. On May 14th, Lewis wrote:

In the evening the men in two of the rear canoes discovered a large brown bear lying in the open grounds about 300 paces from the river, and six of them went out to attack him, all good hunters; they got within 40 paces of him unperceived, two of them reserved their fires [at that time guns could only be fired once before they had to be reloaded] the four others fired nearly at the same time and put each his bullet through him, two of the balls passed through the bulk of both lobes of his lungs, in an instant this monster ran at them with open mouth, the two who had reserved their fir[e]s discharged their pieces at him as he came towards them, boath of them struck him, one only slightly and the other fortunately broke his shoulder, this however only retarded his motion for a moment. The men unable to reload their guns took to flight, the bear pursued and had very nearly overtaken them before they reached the river; two of the party betook themselves to a canoe and the others seperated an[d] concealed themselves among the willows, reloaded their pieces, each discharged his piece at him as they had an opportunity they struck him several times again but the guns served only to direct the bear to them, in this manner he pursued two of them seperately so close that they were obliged to throw aside their guns and pouches and throw themselves into the river altho' the bank was nearly twenty feet perpendicular; so enraged was this animal that he plunged into the river only a few feet behind the second man he had compelled [to] take refuge in the water, when one of those who still remained on shore shot him through the head and finally killed him.

Patrick Gass drew this picture of a similar incident.

British Museum

In June, they found a river which the Indians hadn't told them about, and they didn't know which way to go. Lewis wrote:

to mistake the stream at this period of the season, two months of the traveling season having now elapsed, and to ascend such stream to the rocky Mountain or perhaps much further before we could inform ourselves whether it did approach the Columbia or not, and then be obliged to return and take the other stream would not only loose us the whole of this season but would probably so dishearten the party that it might defeat the expedition altogether . . . the utmost caution was necessary in deciding on the stream to be taken. to this end an investigation of both streams was the first thing to be done; to learn their widths, debths, comparative rappidity of their courants . . . accordingly we dispatched two light canoes with three men in each up those streams; we also sent out several small parties by land with instructions to penetrate the country as far as they conveniently can permitting themselves time to return this evening and indeavour if possible to discover the distant bearing of those rivers by ascending the rising grounds.

They chose the right river; and later in June, the party reached the Great Falls. In the distance, Lewis saw 'the spray arrise above the plain like a collumn of smoke'. Here, the series of waterfalls made it impossible to use the boats; in one spot, Lewis could see 'a sheet of the whitest beaten froath for 200 yards in length and about 80 feet perpendicular'. So the men had to carry the boats and everything in them about 19 miles overland, on an improvised wagon. Clark wrote:

the men has to haul with all their strength wate and art, maney times every man all catching the grass & knobes and stones with their hands to give them more force in drawing on the Canoes and Loads, and notwithstanding the coolness of the air in high presperation and every halt, those not employed in reparing the course, are asleep in a moment, maney limping from the soreness of their feet some become fa[i]nt for a fiew moments, but no man complains all go chearfully on. to state the fatigues of this party would take up more of the journal than other notes which I find scarcely time to set down.

The boats were well-managed; but there was always the danger Lewis wrote about on August 6th:

one of their canoes had just overset and all the baggage wet, the medecine box among other articles and several articles lost a shot pouch and horn with all the implements for one rifle lost and never recovered.

On one occasion two men tried to swim their horses across the river behind a canoe. The canoe struck a tree, and the men were almost drowned, as this picture shows.

British Museum

Abandoning the boats

The headwaters of the Missouri became very shallow; the boats often had to be dragged along. When Lewis and Clark talked with the Snake Indians about the next part of the route, the Indians told them that the streams flowing west (on the opposite side of the Rocky mountains from the Missouri River) were much too steep and dangerous for boats. After looking at the water, Lewis and Clark decided to trade goods such as axes, knives, handkerchiefs and paint to the Indians, in return for horses. But even with horses, the mountains were steep and hard to cross. By September, snow was falling. On September 16th, Clark wrote:

began to Snow about 3 hours before Day and continued all day the Snow in the morning 4 inches deep on the old Snow, and by night we found it from 6 to 8 inches deep, I walked in front to keep the road and found great dificuelty in keeping it as maney places the Snow had entirely filled up the track, and obliged me to hunt Several minits for the track, at 12 oClock we halted on the top of the mountain to worm & dry our Selves a little as well as to let our horses rest and graze a little on Some long grass which I observed, I have been wet and as cold in every part as I ever was in my life.

At the end of September, the expedition had reached a point where the mountains were not so steep, so the rivers were wider, and had fewer rapids. There was timber for building canoes; the horses were left with a group of Indians, for the return journey. The expedition soon took to the water.

Reaching the Pacific

By November, the Pacific was in sight. On November 7th, Clark wrote:

Great joy in camp we are in *view* of the *Oceian*, this great Pacific Octean which we been so long anxious to See.

Lewis and Clark on the Columbia river—a painting made some years later. The artist has partly imagined the scene.

Going back, Lewis and Clark split up for part of the journey, to see whether a slightly easier route could be found. They successfully met again, and on September 23rd, 1806, were back in St. Louis. Only one man had died on the whole journey.

Look at the pictures. What do they tell you about the journey?

What sort of men do you think Lewis and Clark must have been to lead such an expedition successfully? Give reasons for your answer.

What do you think was the most dangerous moment of the expedition? What was the most exciting moment? What was the most difficult decision Lewis and Clark had to make in the course of the journey?

Describe one of these occasions as if you were a member of the expedition telling the tale to a friend afterwards.

Show the main events of the expedition by a set of drawings (pictures or cartoons) with captions.

How do you think Lewis and Clark would advise the President of the U.S.A. about the possibility of developing a trade route along the Columbia and Missouri Rivers?

3 Across the Appalachian Mountains

Towns

When the thirteen colonies declared their independence in 1776, they were well established. Cities flourished; houses were solidly built; schools and colleges had grown; every colony except Delaware and New Jersey had at least one newspaper. A Frenchman, Jean Brissot, who travelled widely in America, published a book in 1791; in it he wrote about Boston:

They have no brilliant monuments, but they have neat and commodious churches, they have good houses, they have superb bridges, and excellent ships. Their streets are well illuminated at night, while many ancient cities of Europe containing proud monuments of art have never thought of preventing the fatal effects of nocturnal darkness.

About Philadelphia, Brissot wrote:

Philadelphia is built on a regular plan; long and large streets cross each other at right angles.
The State-house, where the Legislature assembles, is a handsome building: by its side they are building a magnificent house of justice.
Behind the State-house is a public garden.

This engraving of about 1830 shows Philadelphia from across the river Delaware.

Radio Times Hulton Picture Library

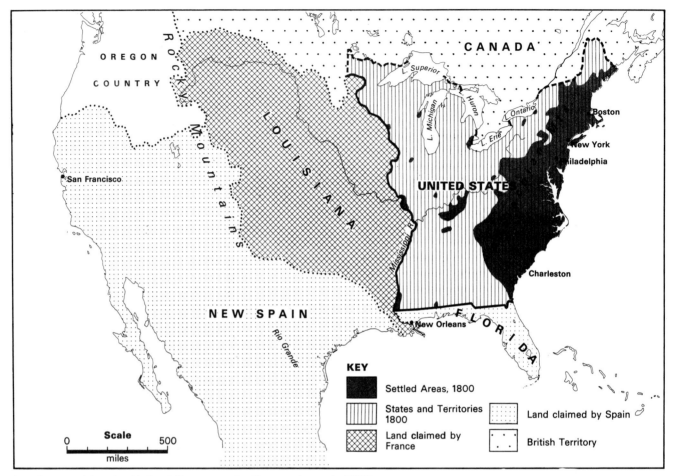

KEY

■	Settled Areas, 1800
▥	States and Territories 1800
▦	Land claimed by France
∴	Land claimed by Spain
·	British Territory

Scale
0 — 500
miles

Land owned by the United States and other nations, in 1800.

When the United States became independent of Britain in 1783, they acquired the land shown on the map above. France and Spain claimed the rest.

You can see from the map that Americans had settled only a small part of the land they owned.

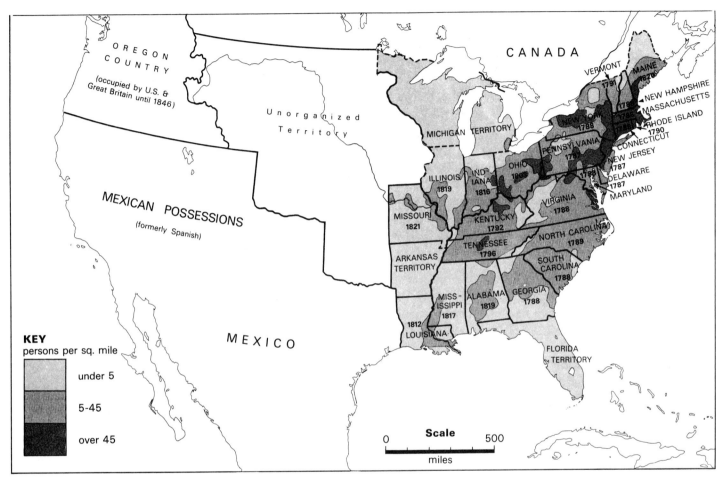

KEY

persons per sq. mile

- under 5
- 5-45
- over 45

Population of the United States by 1830. The States then owned all the land marked 'unorganised territory'. The dates show when each area became a State.

By 1830 many Americans had moved west into the newly organised states and territories. Page 5 in the introduction tells how the states grew.

'Going West'

Townspeople could live comfortably and safely. But adventurous people wanted to explore, and many wanted to find land they could farm for themselves, instead of working for other people all their lives.

While the colonies belonged to Britain, the British government tried to stop settlers moving to the west until proper arrangements had been made with the Indians, who had been living on the land for centuries. But the government found it hard to stop people moving; and after the colonies had declared their independence, more and more settlers started to 'go west'. Benjamin Franklin, an American statesman, pointed out some of the reasons why they wanted to move. In 1784, he wrote:

Land being cheap—from the vast forests still void of inhabitants—hearty young laboring men may easily establish themselves. A little money saved of the good wages they receive while they work for others, enables them to buy the land and begin . . . in which they are assisted by the good will of their neighbours, and some credit. Multitudes of poor people from England, Ireland, Scotland, and Germany, have by this means in a few years become wealthy farmers, who in their own countries, where all the lands are fully occupied, and the wages of labour low, could never have emerged from the mean condition wherein they were born.

Land was cheap, but getting to it was not easy. In 1769, Daniel Boone discovered a way through the Appalachian Mountains, which was called the Cumberland Gap. In 1775, Boone and some axemen cut a rough road through the Cumberland Gap into what is now Kentucky. Settlers followed, hard on his heels. One of them, William Calk, wrote in his diary:

Clearing the wilderness in Pennsylvania

Saturday 8th—We all pack up and started crost Cumberland gap about one o'clock this Day Met a good maney peopel turned Back for fear of the indians but our company goes on Still with good courage.

Fryday 14th—this is a clear morning with a smart frost we go on and have a very miry Road and camp this night on a creek of loral river and are surprised at camp by a wolf.

Thursday 20th—We start early and git down to caintuck to Boons foart about 12 o'clock where we stop they come out to meet us and welcome us with a voley of guns.

Fryday 21st—they begin laying off lots in the town and preparing for people to go to work to make corn.

All the land Calk and his friends were preparing to settle on really belonged to the Cherokee Indians. The Indians didn't like white men ploughing up their land. But more and more land-seeking pioneers poured into what is now Kentucky, Tennessee and Ohio. They built cabins and started to farm. The Indians fought the whites hoping to drive them away.

Hunters and trappers

But some white men had no desire to remain where they first settled. These hunters and trappers tended to put up makeshift cabins, and moved themselves and their families further into the forests whenever neighbours got too near. Hector St. John de Crèvecoeur, who settled in America, wrote a series of 'Letters from an American Farmer', which were published in 1782. He wrote disapprovingly about these wanderers:

It is with men as it is with the plants and animals that grow and live in the forests; they are entirely different from those that live in the plains. By living in or near the woods, their actions are regulated by the wilderness of the neighbourhood. The deer often come to eat their grain, the wolves to destroy their sheep, the bears to kill their hogs, the foxes to catch their poultry. This surrounding hostility immediately puts the gun into their hands; they watch these animals, they kill some; and thus by defending their property, they soon become professed hunters; once hunters, farewell to the plough. The chase renders them ferocious, gloomy, and unsociable; a hunter wants no neighbour, he rather hates them, because he dreads the competition. That new mode of life brings along with it a new set of manners which I cannot easily describe. The manners of the Indian natives are respectable compared with this European medley. Their wives and children live in sloth and inactivity; and having no proper pursuits, you may judge what education the latter receive. Their tender minds have nothing else to contemplate but the example of their parents; like them they grow up a mongrel breed, half civilised, half savage.

This picture, drawn by Frederic Remington, shows what a frontiersman looked like.

Remington Art Memorial Museum, USA

An English traveller, Elias Fordham, wrote in 1818 about the pioneers he had met. His impression was different from Crèvecoeur's. Fordham wrote:

They are unpolished, but hospitable, kind to Strangers, honest and trustworthy. They raise a little Indian corn, pumpkins, hogs, and sometimes have a Cow or two, and two or three horses belonging to each family: But their rifle is their principal means of support. They are the best marksmen in the world. I have spent 7 or 8 weeks with these men, and believe they would sooner give me the last shirt off their backs, than rob me of a charge of powder. Their wars with the Indians have made them vindictive. This class cannot be called first settlers, for they move every year or two.

New settlements

The hunters and trappers were usually quickly followed by people like Calk who wanted to build farms and settle permanently; shopkeepers, lawyers and doctors soon followed them. In 1821, Elijah Iles founded a store in a little village where there were only a dozen or so houses, called Springfield. He explained later how he set about it:

I hunted around and found the stake that had been stuck for the beginning of a town named Springfield, and then bargained for the erection of a store house, to be set near the stake, eighteen feet square, with sheds on the sides for shelter. The house was to be of hewn logs, covered with boards, with heavy poles laid on to keep the boards from blowing off.

I bought my goods at St. Louis. I then chartered a boat on which to ship my goods up the Illinois river to the mouth of the Sangamon, one hundred and fifty miles above St. Louis and within fifty miles of Springfield. The boat was towed up the river by five men walking on shore and pulling a tow line about three hundred feet long. One man on the boat acting as steersman with myself as supercargo, completed the crew.

I believe the boat bringing my goods was the first boat that ever ascended the river, other than Indian-trading boats.

Upon my arrival at Springfield I employed teams to haul the goods. As there were about twenty-five tons of them, it took more than a month to do this, but it was finally accomplished without having the first thing disturbed or missing.

Upon my arrival I found my store house was not quite ready, for the want of nails, and you may believe it was a rough concern; but it answered my purpose. This was the first store house erected

Hudson's Bay Company

This picture shows the sort of house from which some of Iles' customers probably came. Notice how the trees have been killed, by cutting a ring of bark off the trunk. Dead trees were easier to fell than live ones.

in Springfield or in the county, and I was the first one to sell goods in Springfield. For some time my sales were about as much to Indians as to the whites. For the first two years I had no competition, and my customers were widely and thinly scattered.

Iles and his customers did not remain in isolation for very long. Settlers came into Illinois, as they did into Alabama, Mississippi and Georgia. The Indians abandoned their fight; log cabins were replaced by brick buildings; the wilderness had been tamed. People who wanted land of their own to farm now had to travel still further west. (Springfield is now the capital of Illinois.)

Why did some Americans want to 'go west'?

What difficulties were early settlers prepared to face?

If you had been your present age in 1820, would you have wanted your family to go west, or would you rather have lived in Philadelphia or Boston?

What sort of life did the women and children of hunters and trappers lead?

Crèvecoeur and Fordham said different things about the hunters and trappers. Study the accounts and consider what kind of people these hunters and trappers were.

Look at the pictures of Philadelphia. What do you think a frontiersman would miss most, when he left a city to go west?

167

Radio Times Hulton Picture Library

College for orphans, Philadelphia, 1830

24 | THE SETTLEMENT OF THE AMERICAN WEST

4 Travelling east of the Mississippi

When the British troops left the U.S. in 1783, the 'frontier' was really just beyond the Allegheny Mountains. People thought of 'going west' towards the Mississippi, and pioneer families set out into deep forests, to make new homes for themselves. Some families set off in wagons with their cattle walking alongside. Many travelled on foot.

These sketches were drawn by Joshua Shaw, in about 1820.

Chicago Museum of Science and Industry

Look at these pictures and describe how a pioneer family may have spent a day on their journey.

By land

Richer folk travelled in wagons with their servants. But everyone had to ford rivers. Adam Hodgson, travelling in the U.S. and Canada, wrote of what he saw in 1824:

[We] arrived at Line Creek, which, we were told, forms the present boundary between the Creek Nation [Indians] and Alabama. We had travelled that day about forty miles, and had passed as usual many large parties of emigrants, from South Carolina and Georgia, and many gangs of slaves. Indeed, at the edges of the creeks and on the banks of the rivers, we usually found a curious collection of carts, Jersey waggons, heavy waggons, planters, Indians, Negroes, horses, mules, and oxen; the women and little children sitting down frequently for one, two or three, and sometimes five or six hours, to work or play, while the men were engaged in the almost hopeless task of dragging or swimming their vehicles and baggage to the opposite side. Often a light carriage, with a sallow planter and his lady, would bring up the rear of a long cavalcade, and indicate the removal of a family of some wealth, who, allured by the rich lands of Alabama, or the sugar plantations on the Mississippi, had bidden adieu to the scenes of their youth, and undertaken a long and painful pilgrimage through the wilderness.

VT. = VERMONT
N.H. = NEW HAMPSHIRE
MASS. = MASSACHUSETTS
R.I. = RHODE ISLAND
CONN. = CONNECTICUT
N.J. = NEW JERSEY
MD. = MARYLAND
DEL. = DELAWARE

Original Thirteen States

Scale
0 _____ 500
miles

By water

Once across the mountains, some families floated down river for at least part of their journey. Most of them went in 'flatboats'. As you can see from this picture, these boats had cabins on top. A man called Latrobe wrote of one of these boats

The flatboat was an unwieldy box and was broken up, for the lumber it contained, on its arrival at the place of destination. Flatboats had prodigious steering oars, and oars of the same dimensions were hung on fixed pivots on the sides, by which the shapeless and cumbrous contrivance was in some sort managed.

This picture, painted by a Russian, Paul Svinin, who visited the U.S. between 1811 and 1813, shows a flat bottomed scow ferrying passengers across the Susquehanna river.

Metropolitan Museum of Art, New York. Rogers Fund

A flatboat. It was guided by a steering oar at the stern and another at one side.

Radio Times Hulton Picture Library

The Erie Canal

To link the Hudson River with Lake Erie, the Erie Canal was opened in 1825.

This map shows the site of the canal.

Pioneer families often moved more than once. After the Erie Canal was opened, many farming families packed up their goods, travelled along the canal to Buffalo, took a steamer across the lakes and started again in what is now

This engraving shows the Erie Canal near Little Falls.

northern Indiana and Illinois, and southern Michigan and Wisconsin.

Travel on the Erie Canal was slow and not particularly comfortable. Thomas Woodcock, a New York engraver, travelled in a passenger boat in 1836. He wrote:

Radio Times Hulton Picture Library

These boats are about 70 feet long, and with the exception of the Kitchen and bar, is occupied as a Cabin. The forward part being the ladies' Cabin, is separated by a curtain, but at meal times this is removed, and the table is set the whole length of the boat. The Settees that go the whole length of the Boat on each side unfold and form a cot bed. The space between this bed and the ceiling is so divided as to make way for two more. The upper berths are merely frames with sacking bottoms, one side of which has two projecting pins, which fit into sockets in the side of the boat. The other side has two cords attached one to each corner. The bedding is then placed upon them, the space between the berths being barely sufficient for a man to crawl in, and presenting the appearance of so many shelves. These boats have three Horses.

The Bridges on the Canal are very low, particularly the old ones. Every Bridge makes us bend double if seated on anything, and in many cases you have to lie on your back. A young English Woman met with her death a short time since, she having fallen asleep with her head upon a box.

Describe or draw 2 or 3 different ways of travelling over water.

What do you think would be the worst hardships of travelling west in about 1830, by land or water?

If your family had travelled along the Erie Canal to make a new home, what would you have enjoyed about the journey? What would you have disliked?

Write an entry in a diary you might have kept travelling *either* from Georgia to Alabama *or* from New York to Buffalo.

Steamers

Sailing ships were used on the Great Lakes; but steamers operated there after 1818. They also plied up and down the Mississippi; which was far from easy to navigate. Mark Twain, an American writer, apprenticed himself to a river pilot in 1857. He wrote of his experiences:

Steam boats on the Mississippi

If I had really known what I was about to require of my faculties, I should not have had the courage to begin. I supposed that all a pilot had to do was to keep his boat in the river, and I did not consider that that could be much of a trick since it was so wide.

The pilot told Twain to steer close inshore.

Radio Times Hulton Picture Library

I took the wheel, and my heartbeat fluttered up into the hundreds; for it seemed to me that we were about to scrape the side off every ship in the line, we were so close. In half a minute I had a wide margin of safety intervening between the *Paul Jones* and the ships; and within ten seconds more I was set aside in disgrace. When he [the pilot] had cooled a little he told me that the easy water was close ashore and the current outside, and therefore we must hug the bank, upstream. I resolved to be a downstream pilot and leave the upstreaming to people dead to prudence.

They went on up the river. The pilot then asked:

'What's the name of the first point above New Orleans?' I was gratified to be able to answer promptly, and I did. I said I didn't know.
'Don't *know*?'
'Well you're a smart one,' said Mr. Bixby. 'What's the name of the *next* point?'
Once more I didn't know.
'Well, this beats anything. Tell me the name of *any* point or place I told you.'
I studied a while and decided that I couldn't.
'Look-here! What do you start out from, above Twelve-Mile Point, to cross over?'
'I—I—don't know.'
'You—you—don't know?' mimicking my drawling manner of speech. 'What *do* you know?'
'I—I—for nothing, for certain.'
'By the great Caesar's ghost, I believe you. The idea of *you* being a pilot—*you*! Why, you don't know enough to pilot a cow down a lane.'

Roads

Roads outside towns were usually fairly rough. Many were laid out by army officers, others by state and local communities. A Frenchman, Jean Brissot, wrote of a journey he made in 1788:

I set out from Philadelphia for Wilmington, a distance of 28 miles, by a tolerably good road.

The road to Baltimore is frightful, built over clay soil, full of deep ruts, always in the midst of forests, and frequently obstructed by trees uprooted by the wind, which obliges us to seek a new passage among the woods. I cannot conceive why the stage [coach] does not often meet with disaster. Both the drivers and their horses develop great skill and dexterity, being accustomed to these roads. But why are they not repaired? Overseers of the roads are indeed appointed, and fines are sometimes pronounced on delinquencies of this kind; but they are ill collected. Everything is here degraded; it is one of the effects of slavery. The slave works as little as possible; and the master, eager for vile enjoyments, has other concerns than sending his Negroes to repair the roads.

Charles Hoffman travelled in 1833 along the National Road which stretched from Cumberland, through Wheeling and into Illinois, and found it not much better. He wrote:

About thirty miles from Wheeling we first struck the national road. It appears to have been originally constructed of large round stones, thrown without much arrangement on the surface of the soil, after the road was first levelled. These are now being ploughed up, and a thin layer of broken stones is in many places spread over the renovated surface. I hope the roadmakers have not the conscience to call this Macadamizing. It yields like snowdrift to the heavy wheels which traverse it, and the very best parts of the road that I saw are not to be compared with a Long Island turnpike. Two-thirds indeed of the extent traversed were worse than any artificial road I ever travelled, except perhaps the log causeways among the new settlements in northern New York. The ruts are worn so broad and deep by heavy travel, that an army of pigmies might march into the bosom of the country under the cover they would afford.

Poor or not, the roads were well-travelled. An Englishman made notes on a journey he took in 1817. He wrote:

The condition of the people of America is so different from aught that we in Europe have an opportunity of observing that it would be difficult to convey an adequate notion of their character. They are great travelers, and in general, better acquainted with the vast expanse of country spreading over their eighteen states than the English with their little island. They are also a migrating people and even when in prosperous circumstances can contemplate a change of situation which, under our old establishments and fixed habits, none but the most enterprising would venture upon when urged by adversity.

To give an idea of the internal movements of this vast hive, about twelve thousand wagons passed between Baltimore and Philadelphia in the last year, with from four to six horses, carrying from thirty-five to forty hundredweight. Add to these the numerous stages [coaches], loaded to the utmost, and the innumerable travelers on horseback, on foot, and in light wagons, and you have before you a scene of bustle and business, extending over a space of three hundred miles, which is truly wonderful.

What did Mark Twain find so difficult about piloting a boat on the Mississippi?

What was the matter with the early American roads?

Suppose you were the father of a family in 1825. You have decided to take your family to the west. How would you travel? Would you make the same decision, whether you were rich or poor?

What differences did the Englishman writing in 1817 notice between English and American travelling habits?

5 Kit Carson, frontiersman

When Kit Carson was a year old, his family moved to a frontier area in Missouri. Kit grew up knowing how to hunt and shoot; and took part in standing guard against Indian attacks. When he was fifteen, he was apprenticed to a saddler; but as his sister said:

He didn't like it. About the only use he had for a saddle was on a horse's back.

Smithsonian Institution, USA

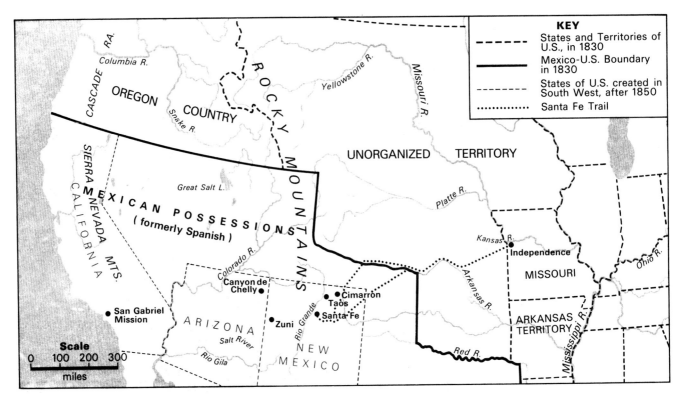

KEY

- – – – States and Territories of U.S. in 1830
- —— Mexico-U.S. Boundary in 1830
- - - - States of U.S. created in South West, after 1850
- ········· Santa Fe Trail

The map shows the American West that Kit Carson knew.

Kit ran away and joined his older brothers who were travelling along the Santa Fe Trail. The saddler put an advertisement in the newspaper:

NOTICE TO WHOM IT MAY CONCERN: That Christopher Carson, a boy about sixteen years old, small for his age, but thickset, light hair, ran away from the subscriber to whome he had been bound to learn the saddler's trade. All persons are notified not to harbor, support or subsist said boy. One cent reward will be given to any person who will bring back said boy.

Santa Fe was in land which belonged to Mexico, and was not then part of the U.S.A. Here Kit met an American, Kincaid, and together they trapped animals for their furs. They stayed for a while in a village or pueblo, the home of the Taos ('Towse') Indians. Pueblo means 'village' in Spanish. The Spaniards were the first Europeans to explore this part of America and several places still have Spanish names.

These are modern pictures of the pueblo, but it looked much the same when Kit Carson saw it. The pueblo is built as it was then of bricks made of mud, baked in the sun. The outside of the building is plastered with more mud. This kind of building is called 'adobe' (out of the mud).

the five story pueblo (village)

Western Ways, Bureau of Indian Affairs, USA

oven for baking bread

Joan Chandler

Kit Carson lived in the valley of the Rio Grande for years and got to know several villages very well. The Taos Indians were a peaceful farming people. They grew crops of maize near each village, and hunted for small animals. The Spanish missionaries had preached Christianity and got the Indians to build churches. This is a photograph of a church built at least two hundred years before Kit Carson reached Taos.

In 1829 Kit Carson was hired to go and trap beaver in the mountains. All trappers were supposed to have a licence, and they were supposed to stay within the boundaries of the U.S. But as Kit Carson recalled when he was telling his life story:

> In those days licences were not granted to citizens of the United States to trap within the limits of the Mexican territory. To avoid all mistrust on the part of the government officers, we traveled in a nothern direction for fifty miles, and then changed our course to southwest, traveled through the country occupied by the Navajo ['Nav-a-ho'] Indians passed the village of Zuni ['Zoo-knee'] and on to the head of the Salt River, one of the tributaries of the Rio Gila [River 'Heel-a'].

At the Salt River, the party was attacked by Apache Indians, but fought them off; then the trappers set out for what is now California. Kit Carson remembered:

> The first four days march was over a country, sandy, burned up, and not a drop of water.

They ran short of food. But eventually they reached the San Gabriel Mission, which the Spaniards had set up many years before, to civilize the Indians in the area. Kit Carson said:

> At the Mission there was one priest, fifteen soldiers,

Mission church at Santo Domingo, a pueblo in the Rio

> and about one thousand Indians. They had about eighty thousand head of stock, fine fields and vineyards, in fact, it was a paradise on earth. We remained one day at the Mission, received good treatment of the inhabitants, and purchased of them what beef we required.

...rande valley. This photograph was taken in 1899.

Smithsonian Institution, USA

The trapping season went well. The party went back to Santa Fe with a very profitable load of furs; and Kit Carson lived the life of a 'mountain man' (see Chapter 6) until about 1842. He married an Indian wife, and they had a daughter. When his wife died he took his daughter to live with his family, in Missouri.

Next he spent a few years as a guide with an expedition sent to map country which trappers and hunters knew, but which had never been explored scientifically.

After this roving life he wanted to settle down. He wrote:

> Dick Owens and I concluded that, as we had rambled enough that it would be advisable for us to go and settle on some good stream and make us a farm. We went to Little Cimarron, built ourselves little huts, put in considerable grain, and commenced getting out timber to enlarge our improvements.

He left the farm to guide another expedition but while he was in California war broke out between the U.S.A. and Mexico. Kit fought with American soldiers against the Mexicans, and after America had won the war again went back to his farm. New Mexico, Arizona and California all became part of the U.S.A.

In 1853 the American government appointed Kit Carson as an Indian Agent in these newly won territories. His job was to report on the Indian tribes in his area, and to try to keep the peace between them and the white settlers. He was a good man for this, because he knew the different tribes well. He described:

> the bold, courageous, marauding Comanche—the wild, treacherous, nomadic Apache—the hardy, industrious agricultural Navajo, or the lazy, degraded, almost brutalized Digger.

The Indians living in pueblos like Taos were fairly peaceable; but other Indians living in what is now New Mexico and Arizona had always been hunters. In 1854, Kit Carson reported to the Governor of the territory:

> The game in the Ute ['youte'] country is becoming scarce, and they are unable to support themselves

KIT CARSON, FRONTIERSMAN | 37

by the chase and hunt, and the government has but one alternative, either to subsist and clothe them or exterminate them.

In 1860, he wrote:

if provisions are not furnished them in sufficient quantities to sustain them during the winter months, they will be reduced to the necessity of thieving and robbing. Their game is being killed or driven off, nothing better can reasonably be expected from them.

The Federal Government built forts, where soldiers were stationed, to deal with the Indians; but some tribes were particularly difficult to subdue. One group, the Navajos, living in what is now Arizona, were very hard to fight because they were shepherds and farmers who lived in family groups. One family would not accept a treaty made with another group; and the country they lived in was hard to travel over, so it was easy to hide from the soldiers.

Because groups of Navajos continued to attack white settlements, the Federal government declared war on the whole tribe; Kit Carson was ordered to go to the Canyon de Chelly and destroy the Navajo crops. In 1864, Kit Carson managed to get into the Canyon; but it was a difficult job. Speaking of it later, he said:

In the walls of the cañons they [the Indians] have regular houses built in the crevices from which they fire and roll down huge stones on an enemy. They have regular fortifications, averaging from one to two hundred feet from the bottom, with portholes for firing. When I captured the Navajos, I first destroyed their crops, and harassed them until the snow fell very deep in the cañons, taking some prisoners occasionally. I took twelve hundred sheep from them at one time, and smaller lots at different times. It took me and three hundred men most of one day to destroy a field of corn (maize).

Left: a modern Navajo, wearing traditional jewellery, standing outside his earth and log hut or hogan.

Right: Navajo country today. At the foot of the cliff is a traditional hogan beside a modern shack.

Bureau of Indian Affairs, USA

 (placed once)

A modern Navajo planting corn in the traditional way

Bureau of Indian Affairs, USA

After this expedition, many Navajos were sent to a reservation miles from their homes; but after a few years they were allowed back into the Canyon de Chelly and the surrounding country. Today, they are the largest Indian tribe in the U.S.; and while many of them have ordinary jobs like white Americans, some still herd sheep and plant maize as their ancestors did before they had heard of Kit Carson. But they no longer fight.

Study the pictures on page 35. Describe the Taos pueblo. How did the Taos Indians make a living?

Look at the pictures of Navajo country. Describe the land and the homes of the people.

In what ways were the Taos and Navajo Indians different from each other? Did they have any customs in common?

What sort of a person was Kit Carson at 16?

Why do you suppose Kit Carson never settled for long as a farmer?

If you had been Kit Carson, which period of his life would you most have enjoyed? Why?

From these extracts, you can see that life in the U.S. changed a good deal during Kit Carson's lifetime. What changes are mentioned here?

6 The Mountain Men

Remington Art Memorial Museum, USA

Frederic Remington drew this picture of two mountain men. He also wrote the caption.

I took ye for an Injun!

A mounted fur trapper with a pack horse

As Lewis and Clark (see Chapter 2) travelled home down the Missouri River, they met two fur trappers coming up. These men were looking for beaver so that they could sell the skins. They were forerunners of the 'mountain men' who travelled far and wide in the West, hunting for beaver.

Trappers

George Ruxton, an Englishman, lived among some of the last of the fur trappers in 1847; he wrote:

Trappers are of two kinds, the 'hired hand' and the 'free trapper': the former hired for the hunt by the fur companies; the latter, supplied with animals and traps by the company, is paid a certain price for his furs.

On starting for a hunt, the trapper fits himself out with the necessary equipment. This equipment consists usually of two or three horses or mules, and six traps. Ammunition, a few pounds of tobacco, dressed deerskins for mocassins, etc., are carried in a wallet of dressed buffalo skin.

Over his left shoulder and under his right arm hang his powderhorn and bullet-pouch. Round the waist is a belt, in which is stuck a large butcher-knife in a sheath of buffalo-hide, made fast to the belt by a chain or guard of steel; which also supports a little buckskin case containing a whetstone. A tomahawk is also often added; and of course a long heavy rifle is part and parcel of his equipment.

As soon as the ice was off the streams, the mountain men set off, singly or in small groups, looking for traces of beaver. Having found them, the trapper:

sets his trap in the run of the animal, hiding it under water, and attaching it by a stout chain to a picket driven in the bank, or to a bush or tree. The trap is baited with the 'medicine', an oily substance obtained from a gland in the beaver. A stick is dipped into this and planted over the trap; and the beaver, attracted by the smell, and wishing a close inspection, very foolishly puts his leg into the trap, and is a 'gone beaver'.

When a lodge is discovered, the trap is set at the edge of the dam, at the point where the animal passes from deep to shoal water, and always under water.

The rendezvous

Beaver were hunted in the spring and autumn, when the furs were best. In the summer, the trappers found their way to the 'rendezvous', a place previously agreed on, where they sold their furs and bought supplies from traders. But it was more than a market. Ruxton writes:

The 'rendezvous' is one continued scene of drunkenness, gambling, and brawling and fighting, as long as the money and credit of the trappers last. Seated round the fires groups are seen with their 'decks' of cards. The stakes are 'beaver', which here is current coin; and when the fur is gone, their horses, mules, rifles and shirts, hunting-packs, and *breeches* are staked. There goes 'hos and beaver!' is the mountain expression when any great loss is sustained; and, sooner or later, 'hos and beaver' invariably find their way into the insatiable pockets of the traders. A trapper often squanders the produce of his hunt, amounting to hundreds of dollars, in a couple of hours.

Dangers

Not all the trappers gambled away their money however. People like Jim Bridger and Kit Carson, who later became an Indian agent (see Chapter 5) saved some of theirs, and used it when they gave up fur trapping. Certainly the trappers earned whatever money they got. Osbourne Russell kept a journal between 1834 and 1843; like other mountain men, he sometimes got lost, in the worst possible conditions; of one occasion he wrote:

After climbing about a mile further we came to large banks of snow 8 or 10 ft. deep and so hard that we were compelled to cut steps with our butcher knives to place our feet in whilst our Mules followed in the same track. These places were from 50 to 200 yards across and so steep that we had to use both hands and feet Dog like in climbing over them.

They were often hungry. Russell remembered:

we were on our way at day break and travelled all day thro' the high Sage and sand down Snake river. We stopped at dark nearly worn out with fatigue, hunger and want of sleep as we had now travelled 65 Mls in two days without eating.

Sometimes it rained:

we spread the Bull skin down in the mud in the dryest place we could find and laid down upon it. We lay tolerably comfortable whilst the skin remained above the surface but the mud being soft the weight of our bodies sunk it by degrees below the water level which ran under us on the skin but we concluded it was best to lie still and keep the water warm that was about us for if we stirred we let in the cold water and if we removed our bed

This engraving, from a drawing by Remington, shows

Mansell Collection

...untain man at a Cree Indian Council, held inside a tepee.

we were more likely to find a worse instead of a better place.

The mountain men had always to be on the lookout for Indians. Some Indians, individually, and some tribes, were friendly. Often mountain men had Indian wives and children. Russell writes:

I cast my eyes down the mountain and discovered 2 Indians approaching within 200 yards of us I immediately aroused my companion who was still sleeping, we grasped our guns they [the Indians] quickly accosted us in the Snake tongue saying they were Shoshonies and friends to the whites, I invited them to approach and sit down then gave them some meat and tobacco. After our visitors had eaten and smoked they pointed out the place where we could descend the mountain.

But others, particularly the Blackfeet, were less approachable. Russell writes:

we were completely surrounded. We cocked our rifles and started thro' their ranks into the woods which seemed to be completely filled with Blackfeet. An arrow struck White on the right hip joint I hastily told him to pull it out and [as] I spoke another arrow struck me in the same place. At length another arrow striking thro' my right leg above the knee benumbed the flesh so that I fell accross a log . . . I . . . kept hopping from log to log thro' a shower of arrows . . . I was very faint from the loss of blood and we set down among the logs determined to kill the two foremost when they came up and then die like men. About 20 of them passed by us within 15 feet without casting a glance towards us and all turning to the right the next minute were out of our sight among the bushes.

THE MOUNTAIN MEN | 45

As the fur trade developed, various trading posts, usually called forts because they could be defended against attack, were set up. Here trappers, Indians and traders met on friendly terms. This picture, painted in 1837, shows various groups inside Fort Laramie, which was first built in 1832 by William Sublette's men. Fort Laramie became an important supply centre on the Oregon Trail.

Walters Art Gallery, USA

Developing the West

The mountain men's lives depended on their being able to find their way about. Ruxton wrote:

Not a hole or corner in the vast wilderness of the 'Far West' but has been ransacked by these hardy men. From the Mississippi to the mouth of the Colarado of the West, from the frozen regions of the North to the Gila in Mexico, the beaver-hunter has set his traps in every creek and stream. All this vast country, but for the daring enterprise of these men, would be even now a *terra incognita* [unknown land] to geographers, as indeed a great portion still [1849] is.

Most of the trappers' knowledge, however, was personal, and was passed on by word of mouth or in sketch maps. One of the army surveyors sent to the west in the 1840s to map it more scientifically, wrote of Jim Bridger:

The builder of Fort Bridger [Bridger built it in 1843] is one of the hardy race of mountain trappers who are now disappearing from the continent, being enclosed in a wave of civilisation. With a buffalo-skin and a piece of charcoal, he will map out any portion of this immense region, and delineate mountains, streams, and the circular valleys called 'holes' with wonderful accuracy.

One of the greatest explorers was Jedidiah Smith.

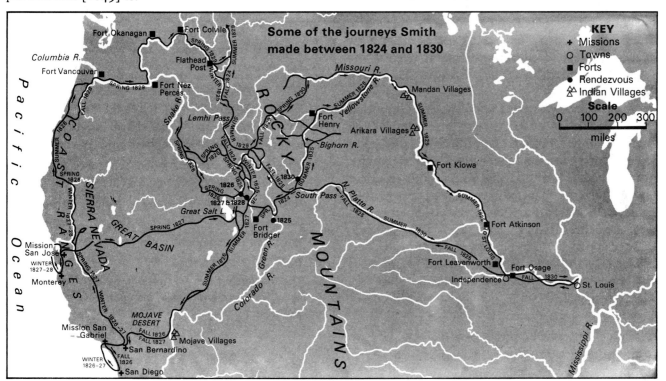

Some of the journeys Smith made between 1824 and 1830

KEY
+ Missions
○ Towns
■ Forts
● Rendezvous
⩜ Indian Villages

Scale
0 100 200 300
miles

Jedidiah Smith was worried by what he saw near Fort Vancouver. He and his partners wrote to the Secretary of War in 1830. Part of the letter read:

Sir: The business commenced some years ago, of taking furs from the United States territory beyond the Rocky Mountains, has since been continued . . . under the firm of Smith, Jackson and Sublette. Packhorses were at first used; but in the beginning of the present year, it was determined to try wagons. [Details of the journey are given]. The usual progress of the wagons was from fifteen to twenty-five miles per day. This is the first time that wagons ever went to the Rocky mountains; and the ease and safety with which it was done prove the facility of communicating overland with the Pacific Ocean. One of the undersigned Jedidiah S. Smith, on his excursion west of the mountains, arrived at the post of the Hudson's Bay Company [a British Company], called Fort Vancouver. At Fort Vancouver the goods for the Indian trade are imported from London, and enter the territories of the United States, paying no duties; and from the same point the furs taken on the other side of the mountains are shipped. To obtain these furs, both trapping and trading are resorted to. In 1824 and 5, they crossed the Rocky mountains, and trapped on the waters of the Missouri river. Thus this territory, being trapped by both parties, is nearly exhausted of beavers; and unless the British can be stopped, will soon be entirely exhausted, and no place left within the United States where beaver fur in any quantity can be obtained.

The object of this communication being to state *facts* to the Government, and to show the facility of crossing the continent to the Great Falls of the Columbia with wagons, and also to show the true nature of the British establishments on the Columbia.

> Jedidiah S. Smith,
> David E. Jackson,
> W. L. Sublette

Within about ten years of this letter, the beaver had indeed almost disappeared. As one trapper complained 'lizards grow poor, and wolves lean against the sand banks to howl'. And fashions changed; men stopped wearing beaver hats, so the demand for furs dropped. The day of the mountain man was over. Jedidiah Smith was later killed by Indians after he had given up trapping beaver.

What do the pictures tell you about the mountain men? What did a trapper need to take with him when he set out to hunt?

What do you suppose the mountain men ate, alone in the mountains for several months as they were?

Imagine yourself taking furs to a rendezvous. Describe to your grandson what happened when you got there.

Which part of a mountain man's life would you have found most exciting? Which most unpleasant?

What were Jedidiah Smith and his partners so concerned about?

What part did the mountain men play in exploring the west?

The fur trappers' life was as wild and free as the cowboys'. Why is the mountain man not so well known, do you think?

7 The Oregon Trail and Californian Miners

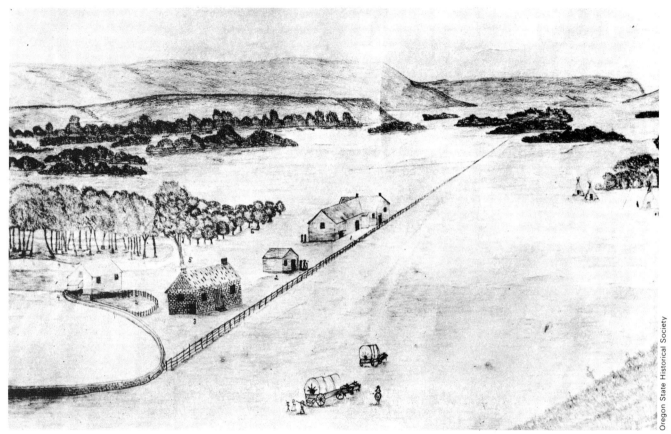

This is a drawing of one of the first mission stations in Oregon.

Oregon State Historical Society

In the 1830s a journey across the United States was very difficult and dangerous. There was no known wagon route, and there were high mountains and deep rivers to cross. But some American missionaries went to work among the Indians living in Oregon. They made the journey overland, and their trip gave hope to other Americans, people who were looking for land to live on.

The Trail

Farmers wanting land of their own in the eastern States were being disappointed. There were too many people; between 1830 and 1840, for instance, Missouri's population grew from about 140,000 to about 383,000. The land west of the Mississippi River had few trees and looked hard to farm; but farmers began to hear that Oregon was lush and green. The idea of travelling to Oregon spread; before long, 'Oregon fever' was a catching disease.

Groups of settlers usually went together, their possessions packed in heavy wagons pulled by oxen. One of the largest groups set out in 1843; there were about 1,000 men, women and children, 120 wagons and several thousand horses and cattle. At first, the whole party travelled together; but the cattle walked so slowly, and took so much guarding, that people who hadn't many animals got impatient. So the group split; Jesse Applegate, who later wrote a book about the journey, was left in charge of the plodding 'cow column'. Applegate described a day's journey:

This map shows the trail most people used to go to Oregon, and Applegate's route.

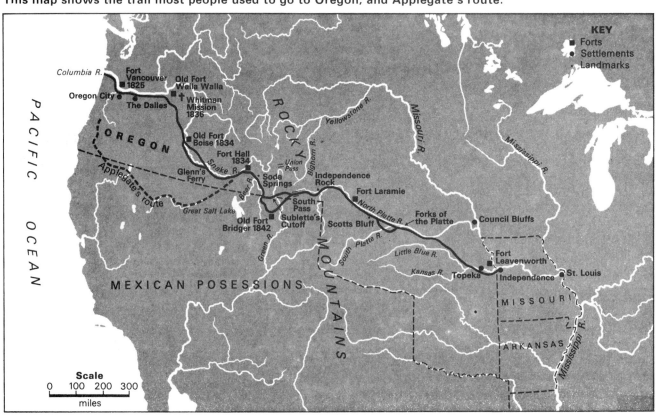

It is 4 A.M.; the sentinels on duty have discharged their rifles—the signal that the hours of sleep are over; and every wagon and tent is pouring forth its night tenants.

Sixty men start from the corral, spreading as they make through the vast herd of cattle and horses that form a semicircle around the encampment, the most distant perhaps two miles away.

In about an hour five thousand animals are close up to the encampment, and the teamsters are busy selecting their teams and driving them inside the 'corral' to be yoked. The corral is a circle one hundred yards deep, formed with wagons connected strongly with each other. It is a strong barrier that the most vicious ox cannot break. From six to seven o'clock is a busy time; breakfast to be eaten, the tents struck, the wagon loaded, and the teams yoked and brought in readiness to be attached to their respective wagons. All know that when, at seven o'clock, the signal to march sounds, those not ready to take their proper places in the line of march must fall into the dusty rear for the day.

This drawing shows wagons grouped as Applegate describes, by Independence Rock.

W.H

Utah State Historical Society

Emigrant train passing Wind River Mountain

There are sixty wagons. They have been divided into fifteen platoons of four wagons each, and each platoon is entitled to lead in its turn. The leading platoon of today will be the rear one tomorrow and will bring up the rear unless some teamster, through indolence or negligence, has lost his place in the line, and is condemned to that uncomfortable post. It is on the stroke of seven: the rushing to and fro, the cracking of the whips, the loud command to oxen, and what seems to be the inextricable confusion of the last ten minutes has ceased. The clear notes of the trumpet sound in the front; the pilot and his guards mount their horses, the leading division of wagons moves out of the encampment and takes up the line of march, the rest fall into their places with the precision of clockwork, until the spot so lately full of life sinks back into the solitude that seems to reign over the broad plain and rushing river, as the caravan draws its lazy length toward the distant El Dorado.

Difficulties

Few people realised how hard the journey would be. Day after day the wagons crawled along, usually covering about 10 or 12 miles.

On the plains it was stiflingly hot; unless it rained heavily. One man travelling in 1844 noted in his diary:

we spent a verry uncomfortable night in all forms of moisture short of swimming.

Cooking in these conditions was unpleasant. The traveller noted:

one young Lady after having kneaded her dough she watched and nursed the fire and held an umbrella over the fire and her skillit [frying-pan] with the greatest composure.

Oregon State Historical Society

Floating wagons down river to the Pacific

The travellers were able to rest for a few days when they reached Fort Laramie (see Chapter 6) where they could buy some supplies and repair their wagons. But they soon had to move on, if they were not to be caught by autumn falls of snow in the Rocky Mountains. This is what happened to a party led by Jacob and George Donner in 1846.

They left the Trail looking for a shorter route and were delayed until deep snows hemmed them into the mountains. Some died from exposure, starving, the rest only survived by cannibalism. For most emigrants the worst part of the journey was the long haul over the Rocky Mountains. When they got to the Columbia river they were able to float the wagons downstream.

Arrival

Some travellers on the trail, particularly small babies, fell ill and died. Some people were killed accidentally; a few were attacked by Indians. But for most immigrants the journey was happier, and most were ready to settle permanently in Oregon when they arrived. Nathaniel Ford, who reached Oregon in 1844, wrote a letter home:

We had a tedious and tiring trip: but I think we are well paid for our trouble; we are in the best country I have ever seen for farming and stock raising. The prairies are easily broken with two yoke of oxen, and harrows up fine for seeding. All the springs and streams are cool and fine flavoured . . . fine view . . . the finest fish.

Gold

Gold was discovered in California in 1848. A clergyman living in a town called Monterey noted what happened:

I have just been conversing with a man who in six days gathered five hundred dollars' worth [of gold]. San Francisco, Sonoma, Santa Cruz, and San José are literally deserted by their inhabitants; all have gone to the gold regions. The farmers have thrown aside their plows, the lawyers their briefs, the doctors their pills, the priests their prayer books, and all are now digging gold.

A very large company left Monterey today for the gold scene, some on horses, some in wagons, some in carts, some on foot, and some on crutches.

By 1849 men were hopefully hurrying to make their fortunes from all over the U.S., and even from abroad. Some sailed round Cape Horn rather than travel over the plains; others set off along the Oregon Trail, only waiting for the winter snow to melt on the prairies. A journalist described the miners' difficulties:

The cholera, ascending the Mississippi from New Orleans, reached St. Louis about the time of their departure from Independence, and overtook them before they were fairly embarked on the wilderness. It is estimated that about four thousand persons perished from this cause. Men were siezed without warning with the most violent symptoms, and instances occurred in which the sufferer was left to die alone by the road-side, while his panic-stricken companions pushed forward, vainly trusting to get beyond the influence of the epidemic.

By the time the companies reached Fort Laramie the epidemic had expended its violence. Now, however, the real hardships of their journey began. Many, who, in their anxiety to get forward with speed, had thrown away a great part of the supplies that encumbered them, now began to want, and were frequently reduced to make use of their mules and horses for food. It was not unusual to kill a quantity of rattlesnakes and have a dish of them, fried, for supper.

Henry E. Huntington Library and Art Gallery, USA

This sketch shows miners cooking over a fire of buffalo 'chips' (dung), as there was no wood on the prairies.

In their haste the miners didn't prepare properly; oxen died, wagons fell apart and goods had to be left by the trail. A man who lived in Salt Lake City, founded in 1847 by a religious group called Mormons, found the trail:

. . . literally strewn with articles that have been thrown away. Bar-iron and steel, crowbars, drills, trunks, spades, ploughs, cooking-stoves without number, kegs, barrels, harness and clothing.

Mining

When the miners reached California, they looked for gold by 'panning'. They dug up a few shovelsful of gravel from a river, put it in a large circular pan or 'washbowl' and swung the pan so that the water and gravel slopped over the edge, leaving the heavier nuggets of gold (if any) behind. But the surface gold was soon picked up; then other methods had to be used.

In many places the surface soil pays when worked in a long-tom. This machine is a trough, generally about twenty feet in length and eight inches in depth, formed of wood, with the exception of six feet at one end, called the 'riddle' which is made of sheet-iron perforated with holes about the size of a large marble. Underneath this colander-like portion of the long-tom is placed another trough, about ten feet long, the sides six inches, perhaps, in height, which, divided through the middle by a slender slat, is called the riffle-box. It takes several persons to manage [properly] a long-tom. Three or four men station themselves with spades at the head of the machine, while at the foot of it stands an individual armed 'wid de shovel an' de hoe'. The spadesmen throw in large quantities of the precious dirt, which is washed down to the riddle by a stream of water leading into the long-tom through wooden gutters of sluices. When the soil reaches the riddle, it is kept constantly in motion by the man with the hoe. Most of the dirt washes over the sides of the riffle-box, but the gold, being so astonishingly heavy, remains safely at the bottom of it. Many of the miners decline washing the top dirt at all, but try to reach as quickly as possible the bed-rock, where are found the richest deposits of gold.

When a company wish to reach the bed-rock as quickly as possible, they sink a shaft [which is nothing more nor less than digging a well] until they 'strike it'. They then commence drifting

Some men in this drawing are panning gold. Others, like the three in the left foreground are using a 'cradle'. A cradle was a wooden box, which could be rocked back and forth. It held more gravel than a pan.

Radio Times Hulton Picture Library

coyote-holes, as they call them, in search of crevices, which often pay immensely. These coyote-holes sometimes extend hundreds of feet into the side of the hill.

Some miners got rich. Many more found nothing; some couldn't even find a place to dig. A song went:

When I got there, the mining ground
Was staked and claimed for miles around,
And not a bed was to be found,
   When I went off to prospect.
The town was crowded full of folks,
Which made me think 'twas not a hoax;
At my expense they cracked their jokes,
   When I was nearly starving.

The gold which could be easily mined was soon exhausted. It became necessary to use machinery to crush rock, or to cut into it with water from a high pressure hose. Men were employed by companies to mine, rather than doing it on their own.

California was not the only place where gold was found. Silver, copper and other metals were discovered in other western States. Each new strike brought hordes of fortune hunters. Brigham Young, the Mormon leader, thought little of miners. He said:

Whenever I see a man going along with an old mule that can hardly stand up, and a frying pan and an old quilt, I say 'There goes a millionaire in prospect.' These millionaires are all over the country. And they haven't a sixpence.

Sometimes mining operations went on in the same place for long enough to allow a town to grow up, which remained when the metal played out. More often, when the mining stopped, the town collapsed; only the ghosts were left.

What kind of person do you think you would have to be, to set out on the Oregon Trail?

What made the journey worthwhile?

Imagine you travelled along the Trail with your family when you were a child. Tell your own children what a day on the Trail was like.

If you were setting out on the Trail, what sort of things would you pack in your wagon? What do you think you would most have hated to leave behind, if you had been a father? a mother? yourself?

How did miners search for their gold?

What hardships did the miners face?

Suppose you had gone to the goldfields in 1849, but had had little luck. What would you have done next?

How do you think miners contributed to the settlement of the U.S.?

8 The Plains Indians

Many different groups of Indians lived in America long before any white men arrived. One group, split into many tribes, lived on the rolling, grassy plains west of the Mississippi. An American artist, Catlin, travelled west in the 1830s especially to paint these plains Indians.

Catlin drew a map, on which the map below is based, showing where some of the tribes lived.

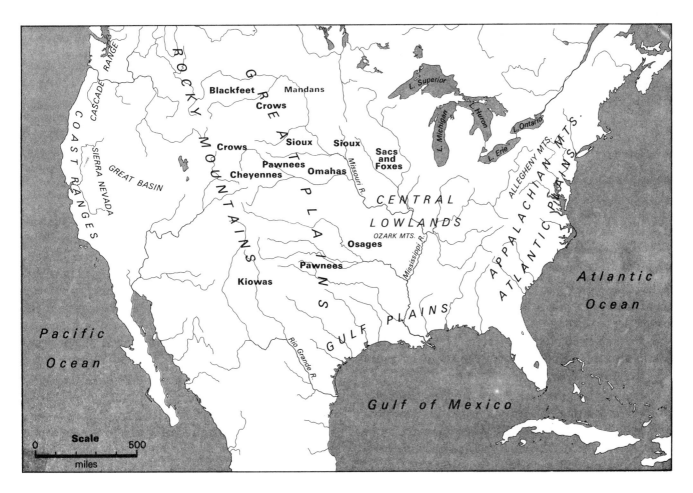

Buffalo

The Indians lived on buffalo; huge herds of these animals roamed the prairie.

A Spanish traveller wrote in 1540:

With the skins they make their houses, with the skins they clothe and shoe themselves, of the skins they make rope, and also of the wool; from the sinews they make thread, with which they sew their clothes and also their houses; from the bones they make awls; the dung serves them for wood, because there is nothing else in that country; the stomachs serve them for pitchers and vessels from which they drink; they live on the flesh.

A buffalo hunt

A scientist named Grinnell lived for a time with the Pawnee tribe; in 1872 he went with them on a buffalo hunt. The Pawnees, by this time, were living on a reservation, but they were allowed to visit a buffalo range twice each year. The hunt was conducted as it always had been. Grinnell described the ceremony which preceded the hunt:

The village seemed deserted, but off toward the medicine lodge, which stood upon its outskirts, I could see a throng of Indians. The ceremonies which comprised the consecration of the buffalo staves and the buffalo dance, were about to begin. The great dirt lodge was crowded.

For several days the priests and doctors had been preparing for this. At first their voices were low and mumbling, but gradually they became more earnest and lifted their eyes toward heaven. Now and then disjointed sentences reached me. 'Father, you are the Ruler — We are poor — Take pity on us — Send us plenty of buffalo, plenty of fat cows — Father, we are your children — help the people — send us plenty of meat, so that we may be strong, and our bodies may increase and our flesh grow hard — Father, you see us, listen.' As they prayed they moved their hands backward and forward over the implements which they held, and at length reverently deposited them on the ground within the line of buffalo skulls, and then stepped back, still continuing their prayers.

After the prayers, a buffalo dance was held, which lasted three days.

The hunt itself was guided by twenty-four warriors; it was important that the buffalo should not be frightened before the tribe could surround the herd. Scouts, sent ahead of the main tribe, galloped back when they had sighted a herd of buffalo.

The scene that we now beheld was such as might have been witnessed here a hundred years ago. Here were eight hundred warriors, stark naked, and mounted on naked animals. A strip of rawhide, or a lariat, knotted about the lower jaw, was all their horses' furniture. Among all these men there was not a gun nor a pistol, nor any indication that they had ever met with the white men. Their bows and arrows they held in their hands.

As we proceeded, the pace became gradually a little more rapid. The horses went along easily and without effort. Each naked Indian seemed a part of his steed, and rose and fell with it in the rhythmic swing of its stride. Gradually the slow gallop became a fast one.

This is a picture, drawn by Catlin, of Mandan Indians performing the Buffalo dance. The dance was part of their religious ceremonies. Notice that these Mandan Indians did not live in portable wigwams, but in earth lodges. The Mandans were farmers, as well as buffalo hunters.

We were again halted. Two of the soldiers recon-noitered, and then signalled that the buffalo were in sight. As we rode slowly up over the ridge, we saw spread out before us a wide valley black with buffalo. Two miles away, on the other side, rose steep ragged bluffs, up which the clumsy buffalo would make but slow progress, while the ponies could run there nearly as fast as on level ground. It was the very place that would have been chosen for a surround.

At least a thousand buffalo were lying down in the midst of this amphitheater. Some of the outlying bulls seemed to observe us, and after looking for a moment or two, these started in rapid flight. This attracted the attraction of the herd, and when we were yet half a mile from them, they took the alarm. At once all were on their feet. For a moment they gazed bewildered at the dark line that was sweeping toward them, and then, down went every huge head and up flew every little tail, and the herd was off in a headlong stampede for the opposite hills. The oldest man of the soldiers turned back toward us, and uttered a shrill *Loo-ah*! It was the word we had waited for.

Like an arrow from a bow each horse darted for-ward. Now all restraint was removed, and each man might do his best. What had been only a wild gallop became a mad race. Each rider hoped to be the first to reach the top of the opposite ridge, and to turn the buffalo back into the valley, so that the surround might be completely successful. How swift those little ponies were, and how admirably the Indians managed to get out of them all their speed! I had not gone much more than half-way across the valley when I saw the leading Indians pass the

Hunting buffalo was dangerous, as this picture shows, but

head of the herd, and begin to turn the buffalo.

Back came the herd, and I soon found myself in the midst of a throng of buffalo, horses and Indians. There was no yelling nor shouting on the part of the men, but their stern set faces, and the fierce gleam of their eyes, told of the fires of excitement

e Indians lived on them. The drawing is by George Catlin.

Mansell Collection

that were burning within them. It was far more interesting to watch the scene than to take part in it, and I soon rode to a little knoll from which I could overlook the whole plain. Many brown bodies lay stretched upon the ground, and many more were dashing here and there closely attended by relentless pursuers. It was sad to see so much death, but the people must have food, and none of this meat would be wasted.

Why did the Plains Indians hunt the buffalo? This writer, Grinnell, evidently admired the Pawnees. What for?

Belief

To the plains Indian, it was clear that 'No man can succeed in life alone, and he cannot get the help he wants from men; therefore he seeks help through some bird or animal which Wakan'tanka sends for his assistance.' In solitude, each youth sought a vision, by fasting and keeping vigils. When he had his vision, he made a song about it. A Sioux song is:

At night may I roam
Against the winds may I roam
At night may I roam
When the owl is hooting
May I roam.

At dawn may I roam
Against the winds may I roam
At dawn may I roam
When the crow is calling
May I roam.

Attitudes to white men

The earliest contacts with white men were often friendly. The mountain men (see Chapter 6) in particular, got on well with most tribes. But times changed. An old trapper explained his viewpoint to a journalist, Chisholm, in 1868:

When I travelled this country twenty years ago there was no trouble with the Indians. I have been all through their camps, the Blackfeet, the Sioux and the Crows, and I turned my horse out and lay down at night with just as little fear as I would in St. Louis or any big city—and a d—— sight less. When I came across their camps they treated me to the best they had. They gave me the best supper they could set down, and they let me have as many Buffalo skins to sleep on as would smother me. Now these same Indians, if I got near them would scalp me.

White buffalo hunters slaughtered huge numbers of the animals to sell the hides in the East, leaving the carcasses to rot. Black Elk, a Sioux holy man, spoke of the coming of the white men between 1863 and 1890. (Bison are buffalo.)

Once we were happy in our own country and we were seldom hungry for then the two-leggeds and the four-leggeds lived together like relatives, and there was plenty for them and for us. But the Wasichus [white men] came.

I was ten years old that winter [1873] and that was the first time I ever saw a Wasichu. At first I thought they all looked sick.

That fall [1883], they say, the last of the bison herd was slaughtered by the Wasichus. I can remember when the bison were so many that they could not be counted, but more and more Wasichus came to kill them until there were only heaps of bones scattered where they used to be. The Wasichus did not kill them to eat; they killed them for the metal that makes them crazy, and they took only the hides to sell. Sometimes they did not even take the hides, only the tongues; and I have heard that fireboats came down the Missouri loaded with dried bison tongues. You can see that the men who did this were crazy.

As they saw their way of life being destroyed, the Indians attacked the whites wherever they could. Government troops were sent to subdue the tribes. The soldiers often treated the Indians cruelly as Lieutenant Cramer tells of the Sand Creek massacre (1864):

We arrived at the Indian village about daylight. Colonel Chivington moved his regiment to the front, the Indians retreating up the creek, and hiding under the banks. White Antelope ran towards our columns unarmed, and with both arms raised, but was killed. Several other of the warriors were killed in like manner. The women and children were huddled together, and most of our fire was concentrated on them. The Indian warriors, about one hundred in number, fought desperately; there were about five hundred all told. I estimated the loss of the Indians to be from one hundred and twenty-five to one hundred and seventy-five killed; no wounded fell into our hands and all the dead were scalped. The Indian who was pointed out as White Antelope had his fingers cut off. Our force was so large that there was no necessity of firing on the Indians. They did not return the fire until after our troops had fired several rounds. I told Colonel Chivington that it would be murder, in every sense of the word, if he attacked those Indians. His reply was, bringing his fist down close to my face, 'Damn any man who sympathizes with Indians'. He had come to kill Indians and believed it to be honorable to kill Indians under any and all circumstances.

Tribe by tribe, the Indians were conquered; surrender was bitter. This is the surrender speech of Chief Joseph of the Nez Perce tribe, in 1877.

I am tired of fighting. Our chiefs are killed. Looking Glass is dead. The old men are all killed. It is the young men who say yes or no. He who led the young men is dead. It is cold and we have no blankets. The little children are freezing to death. My people, some of them, have run away to the hills, and have no blankets, no food; no one knows where they are, perhaps freezing to death. I want time to look for my children and see how many of them I can find. Maybe I shall find them among the dead. Hear me, my chiefs, I am tired; my heart is sick and sad. From where the sun now stands I will fight no more forever.

Chief Joseph

This picture is of Sitting Bull, a Sioux chief, and some of his family after they were taken prisoner.

This was Sitting Bull's last song.

> A warrior
> I have been.
> Now
> It is all over.
> A hard time
> I have.

How did the destruction of the buffalo affect the Plains Indians?

Why did the Indians gradually become hostile to white men?

Had you been a white settler looking for land in the 1860s, would you have been sympathetic to the Indians or would you have wanted them out of your way?

9 Farming on the great plains

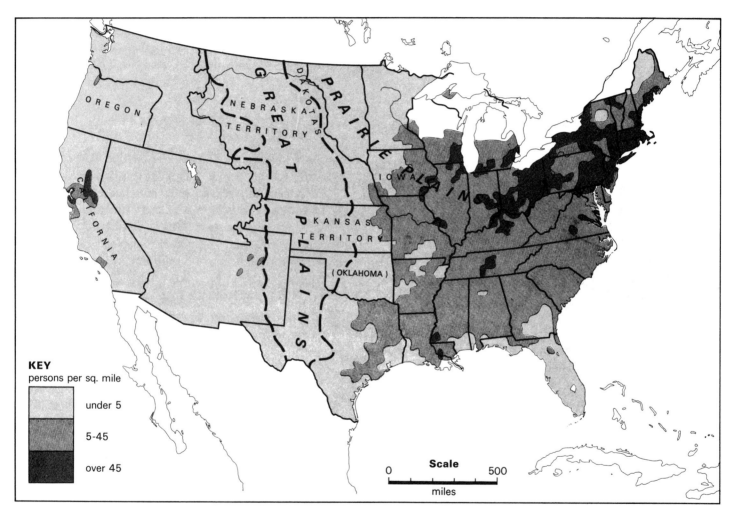

KEY

persons per sq. mile

under 5

5-45

over 45

Scale

0   500

miles

This map shows you the plains, and the areas of settlement in the U.S., in about **1860**.

The plains

When pioneer farmers, looking for land, thought about the plains, they were not anxious to settle there. How could a man build a house or fence his land, when there were few trees to provide wood? How could a farmer raise crops without water? While there was empty land in California and Oregon, it was easier just to travel across the plains, and leave this strange place to the troublesome Indians. Writing about the plains in 1860, a man who knew them well stated:

You look on, on, on, out into space, out almost beyond time itself. You see nothing but the rise and swell of land and grass, and then more grass — the monotonous, endless prairie! A stranger traveling on the prairie would get his hopes up, expecting to see something different on making the next rise. To him the disappointment and monotony were terrible. 'He's got loneliness', we would say of such a man.

Why was land on the plains difficult to farm?

What was frightening about the plains?

During the 1860s, good farming land elsewhere was becoming hard to find, so settlers began to consider how they could make use of this strange country.

There were no old tree stumps or boulders to get in the way of ploughs and reapers; and many farmers set out, as Hamlin Garland's father did, to make farms in the prairie. Hamlin Garland remembered being taken to Iowa; he wrote about it in his autobiography: *A Son of the Middle Border.*

Each mile took us farther and farther into the unsettled prairie until in the afternoon of the second day, we came to a meadow so wide that its western rim touched the sky without revealing a sign of man's habitation other than the road in which we travelled.

The plain was covered with grass tall as ripe wheat and when my father stopped his team (of horses pulling the wagon) and came back to us and said, 'Well, children, here we are on The Big Prairie', we looked about us with awe.

Wheat

Wheat grew well on the prairies, Hamlin Garland remembered:

As I look back over my life on that Iowa farm the song of the reaper fills a large place in my mind. We were all worshippers of wheat in those days. The men thought and talked of little else between seeding and harvest, and you will not wonder at this if you have known and bowed down before such abundance as we then enjoyed.

Reaping generally came about the 20th of July, the hottest and dryest part of the summer, and was the most pressing work of the year. It demanded early rising for the men, and it meant an all day broiling over the kitchen stove for the women. On many days the mercury mounted to ninety-five in the shade, but with wide fields all yellowing at the same moment, no one thought of laying off. A storm might sweep it flat, or if neglected too long, it might 'crinkle'.

Farm work was hard and monotonous. Hamlin Garland remembered the excitement the circus brought:

From the time the 'advance man' flung his highly colored posters over the fence till the coming of the glorious day we thought of little else. It was Indian and Arabia and the jungle to us.

I here pay tribute to the men who brought these marvels to my eyes. To rob me of my memories of the circus would leave me as poor as those to whom life was a drab and hopeless round of toil. In one day—in part of one day—we gained a thousand new conceptions of the world and of human nature. We always went home wearied with excitement, and dusty and fretful—but content. We had seen it. Next day as we resumed work in the field the memory of its splendors went with us like a golden cloud.

Settlers moved quickly into the plains during the 1870s and 1880s. Hamlin Garland watched the change.

The early seventies were years of swift change on the Middle Border. Day by day the settlement thickened. Section by section the prairie was blackened by the plow. Month by month the sweet wild meadows were fenced and pastured and so at last the colts and cows all came into captivity. Lanes of barbed wire replaced the winding wagon trails, groves of Lombardy poplar and European larch replaced the towheads of aspen and hazel through which we had pursued the wolf and fox.

A reaping machine, 1880

Radio Times Hulton Picture Library

Houses

Howard Rueda, a settler in Kansas, wrote a letter in 1877 describing his home. ('Corn' is maize.)

This is a sod house, plastered inside. The sod wall is about 2 feet thick at the ground, and slopes off on the outside to about 14 inches at the top. The roof is composed of a ridge pole and rafters of rough split logs, on which is laid corn stalks, and on top of those are two layers of sod. The roof has a very slight pitch, for if it had more, the sod would wash off when there is a heavy rain.

When the prairie is thoroughly soaked by rain or snow is the best time for breaking sod for building. The regulation thickness is $2\frac{1}{2}$ inches.

The door and window frames are set in place first and the wall built around them. Building such a house is hard work.

Grasshoppers

Glidden took out a patent for barbed wire in 1874 (see Chapter 12). Sales boomed, because the wire could be used instead of wood for fencing. But although the settlers had found new ways of building houses and a new material for making fences, they were not prepared for a new sort of insect. Stuart Henry wrote down his memories of farming in Kansas:

In 1874 came a gigantic calamity in the form of a raid of grasshoppers which ate up every bit of green vegetation from the Rocky Mountain to and beyond the Missouri River. I recall that when coming home late one afternoon for supper I stepped back surprised to see what became known as Rocky Mountain locusts covering the side of the house.

As there were few trees on the plains, settlers built houses shows a family outside their sod house.

from lumps of earth cut out of the prairie. This picture

Already inside, they feasted on the curtains. People set about killing them to save gardens, but this soon proved ridiculous. Specially contrived machines, pushed by horses, scooped up the hoppers in grain fields by the barrelful to burn them. This, too, was then nonsensical. Vast hordes, myriads. In a week grain fields, gardens, shrubs, vines, had been eaten down to the ground or to the bark. Nothing could be done. You sat by and saw everything go.

Then there was a drought.

Even wives who had had a little pardonable vanity left quit trying to save their complexions. They let their tresses go dry and stick out any way. The story was told of seeing on a street a woman in a garment she had sewed together from the halves of different flour sacks, without taking the pains to remove their brands.

What with federal and other public aid, the population lived through the great grasshopper year mainly from necessity as well as pluck. It was a close call. But the locusts or a drought or both the next year would practically wipe out this early folk. A mighty and unexpected blessing, however, intervened. Since low and moister regions than the Rocky Mountains cause its grasshopper progeny to die before maturity, one raid will not continue elsewhere its severest damage into the following years. This is what took place in the plains in the spring of 1875, though that could not have been foreseen by the disheartened people.

Also the seed grain supplied by Eastern charity made good, and the fortunate season in 1875 brought ample crops to meet good prices.

The Federal government gave huge blocks of land to railway companies so that the companies would build railways to places where settlers had not yet gone. The railway companies needed customers; so they sold the land. **They put out advertisements in the eastern U.S. even in Europe, like this one.**

B & M R LAND ADVERTISING CIRCULAR - 1873

During the 1870s and 1880s hundreds of thousands of farmers streamed into Kansas, Nebraska and the Dakotas. But the insects, drought and low prices for farm produce, drove many of the settlers back east. The editor of the *Gazette* (Kansas) wrote in 1895:

There came through yesterday two old-fashioned mover wagons headed east. The stock in the caravan would invoice four horses, very poor and very tired, one mule, more disheartened than the horses, and one sad-eyed dog. A few farm implements of the simpler sort were loaded in the wagon, but nothing that had wheels was moving except the two wagons. All the rest of the impedimenta had been left on the battlefield, and these poor stragglers, defeated but not conquered, were fleeing to another field, to try the fight again. For ten years they had been fighting the elements. They have tossed through hot nights, wild with worry, and have arisen only to find their worst nightmares grazing in reality on the brown stubble in front of their sun-warped doors. They had such high hopes when they went out there.

Oklahoma

Some settlers gave up and went back east. But others took their places on the plains. During the 1880s settlers occupied most of the best land there. Until then, what is now Oklahoma had been reserved for the Indian tribes; but settlers pressed the Federal government to open at least part of the Territory for white people. The President gave way. To keep out settlers until it was time for them to go in, troops were stationed along the border; almost 100,000 people lined up waiting for the signal to be given at midday on April 22nd, 1889.

A man who took part in the rush, chose to travel by train scheduled to stop at a place called Guthrie. He wrote:

And now the hour of twelve was at hand. Suddenly the air was pierced with the blast of a bugle. Hundreds of throats echoed the sound. The saddled steeds bounded forward; and wagons and carriages and buggies and prairie schooners and a whole congregation of curious equipages joined in this unparalleled race, where every starter was bound to win a prize.

Settlers racing for land

Oklahoma Historical Society

One old white-bearded fellow especially commanded attention. He was mounted on a coal-black thoroughbred, and avoided any disaster by checking the pace of his animal when ravines had to be crossed. But his splendid bursts of speed when no obstructions barred the way, soon placed him far in advance of all his competitors.

Our train was one of the participants in this un-exampled race, and, while watching the scurrying horsemen, we ourselves had been gliding through the landscape. All that there was of Guthrie at 1:30 P.M., when the first train unloaded its first instalment of settlers, was a water-tank, a small station-house, a shanty for the Wells, Fargo Express [a stage-coach firm] and a Government Land Office, hastily constructed five hundred feet from the depot.

I remember throwing my blankets out of the car window the instant the train stopped at the station. Then I joined the wild scramble for a town lot up the sloping hillside. There were several thousand people converging on the same plot of ground, each eager for a town lot which was to be acquired without cost or without price.

I found myself, without exactly knowing how, about midway between the government building and depot. It occurred to me that a street would probably run past the depot. I accosted a man who looked like a deputy, and asked him if this was to be a street along here.

'Yes', he replied, 'We are laying off four corner lots right here for a lumber yard.'

'Is this the corner where I stand?' I inquired.

'Yes,' he responded, approaching me.

'Then I claim this corner lot!' I said with decision, as I jammed my location stick in the ground and hammered it securely home with my heel. 'I propose to have one lot at all hazards on this town site, and you will have to limit yourself to three, in this location at least.'

Ten thousand people had 'squatted' upon a square mile of prairie that first afternoon. Here indeed was *a city laid out and populated in half a day.*

What do the pictures tell you about life on the prairie?

How did people first build houses on the prairie?

Would you have stayed in Kansas, had you been trying to farm there in 1874? Write a discussion you and your wife/husband would have had, deciding whether to go or stay.

What defeated some settlers on the plains, and made them move back east?

How do you account for the difference between Hamlin Garland's arrival in Iowa, and the scramble into Guthrie?

Would you have settled on the plains, if that was the only way you could have had your own land? Give reasons for your answer.

10 Cowboys

In 1865, wild 'longhorn' cattle were worth about 5 dollars each in Texas, where there were a great many of them, and about 50 dollars a head in other parts of the country where people needed beef. It seemed easy to make a fortune; all one had to do was to round up some wild cattle and drive them 1,000 miles or so to market, letting them graze on the way. So the 'long drive' began.

This picture gives some idea of what a long drive looked like.

University of Texas

The cook's wagon

Andy Adams wrote a book called *The Log of a Cowboy*, describing his first trip herding cattle. There were 13 cowboys, a man to look after their horses (every cowboy had ten horses), and a cook, to drive 3,000 cattle. Flood was the name of the foreman. Andy Adams describes the trail:

With six men on each side, and the herd strung out for three-quarters of a mile, it could only be compared to some mythical serpent or Chinese dragon, as it moved forward on its sinuous, snail-like course.

Two riders, known as point men, rode out and well back from the lead cattle, and by riding forward and closing in as occasion required, directed the course of the herd. The main body of the herd trailed along behind the leaders like an army in loose marching order, guarded by outriders, known as swing men, who rode well out from the advancing column, warding off range cattle and seeing that none of the herd wandered away or dropped out. There was no driving to do; the cattle moved of their own free will as in ordinary travel. Flood seldom gave orders; but, as a number of us had never worked on the trail before, at breakfast on the morning of our start he gave these general directions:

'From the moment you let them off the bed ground in the morning until they are bedded at night, never let a cow take a step, except in the direction of its destination. In this manner you can loaf away the day, and cover from fifteen to twenty miles, and the herd in the mean time will enjoy all the freedom of an open range. Of course, it's long, tiresome hours to the men; but the condition of the herd and saddle stock demands sacrifices on our part, if any have to be made. And I want to caution you younger boys about your horses; there is such a thing as having ten horses in your string, and at the same time being afoot. Accidents will happen to horses, but don't let it be your fault.'

Living conditions on the trail were simple. Bedding, food and cooking pots were carried in the cook's wagon. The cook lit a fire of buffalo 'chips' (dung) each morning, before daybreak, and cooked meat, coffee, and a sort of bread. He packed his wagon after the herd had started along the trail, caught it up, and started cooking again ahead of the herd where the foreman decided to stop for the night. There were no beds. Andy Adams noted:

We had two pairs of blankets each, which, with an ordinary wagon sheet doubled for a tarpaulin, and coats and boots for pillows, completed our couch. We slept otherwise in our clothing worn during the day.

But few nights were peaceful. Each night the foreman tried to see that the herd stopped near water so that the cattle could drink; he hoped they would lie down and sleep. All night, taking it in turns, two cowboys rode round the herd, whistling or singing to reassure the animals; but the cattle were easily frightened and ready to leap to their feet and run away. Once a stampede started, the cowboys had to try to avoid losing all the cattle. James Cook, a cowboy, wrote about the problem:

There was little use trying to stop a stampede when the herd presented too wide a front. The great mass of the frightened animals following in the wake of the leaders would, by their weight alone, force the leaders over any obstacle which they might encounter. Over bluffs and banks they would go, piling up when the fall was great, not without some broken necks, backs, or limbs. After running for perhaps half a mile, the herd would have become strung out, the strongest and fleetest having forged to the front.

As soon as the herd was sufficiently strung out, the riders would try to get near the lead cattle and if possible swing or turn them, so that they would circle back into the mass of cattle following. This was done by crowding along one side of the leaders, the cowboys yelling and singing to them. This would force the cattle into a compact bunch again, all running in a circle, or 'milling'.

James Cook saw a friend killed on one of these stampedes. Andy Adams' account of his first stampede shows why. (Priest and Officer are names of other cowboys; 'mesquite' is a sort of prickly shrub which grows in Texas and else-where.)

All sounds were submerged by the general din; and I was only brought to the consciousness that I was not alone by seeing several distinct flashes from sixshooters on my left, and, realizing that I also had a gun, fired several times in the air in reply. I was soon joined by Priest and Officer, and the three of us held together some little distance, for it would have been useless to attempt to check or turn this onslaught of cattle in their first mad rush.

Suddenly in the dark we encountered a mesquite thicket into which the lead cattle tore with a crashing of brush and a rattle of horns that sent a chill up and down my spine. But there was no time to hesitate for our horses were in the thicket, and with the herd closing in on us there was no alternative but to go through it, every man for himself.

A stampede was a frightening situation, as this picture by Frederic Remington shows.

The cattle scattered, but a bunch followed Andy Adams. He lost Priest and Officer in the darkness, but another cowboy caught him up. This cowboy and Adams tried to control their bit of the herd.

Remington Art Memorial Museum

There were about fifty or sixty big steers in the lead of our bunch, and, after worrying them into a trot, we opened in their front with our sixshooters, shooting into the ground in their very faces, and were rewarded by having them turn tail and head the other way. Taking advantage of the moment, we jumped our horses on the retreating leaders, and as fast as the rear cattle forged forward, easily turned them. . . . We soon had a mill going which kept them busy, and rested our horses. Once we had them milling, our trouble, as far as running was concerned, was over, for all two of us could hope to do was to let them exhaust themselves in this endless circle.

It then lacked an hour of daybreak, and all we could do was to ride around and wait for daylight.

When the sun was sufficiently high to scatter the mists which hung in clouds, there was not an object in sight by which we could determine our location. . . .

They finally found their way, with their cattle, to the foreman; who immediately sent Adams out to look for another group of animals. Adams found another two cowboys.

Both of them cursed me roundly for not bringing them a canteen of water, though they were well aware that in an emergency like the present, our foreman would never give a thought to anything but the recovery of the herd. Our comfort was nothing; men were cheap, but cattle cost money.

What was the job of the 'point' and the 'swing' men?

Write a story about a dangerous stampede.

Cook wrote of what happened when the beast was lassoed.

The horse then came to a sudden stop, and the rider jumped off and, with one of the short 'tie-ropes' which he always carried tucked under his belt, 'hog-tied' the bull, cow, or whatever age or sex of cow brute he had thrown. This had to be done quickly, before the animal could recover from the shock of the fall. The animals did not mind running from a man ten or twenty miles, but when brought to bay by this treatment, their rage would be such that a man would have to take great and sudden care if he valued his life. It would be horns versus pistol should a strong animal regain its feet before its pursuer could tie it down or, failing, be unable to get back into his saddle.

To survive, a cowboy had to be an expert horseman. He had to have other skills too, as this picture shows.

Sometimes cattle had to be taken across rivers as this photograph shows. Cattle and horses, sometimes even a cowboy, were drowned.

Often there was too little water. Andy Adams remembered a terrible time when there was no water in the streams the foreman had depended on. For three days the cattle had walked without drinking. Andy Adams wrote:

Good cloudy weather would have saved us, but in its stead was a sultry morning without a breath of air, which bespoke another day of sizzling heat. We had not been on the trail over two hours before the heat became almost unbearable to man and beast. The lead cattle turned back several times, wandering aimlessly in any direction, and it was with considerable difficulty that the herd could be held on the trail . . . they finally turned back over the trail, and the utmost efforts of every man in the outfit failed to check them. We drew our ropes in their faces, and when this failed, we resorted to shooting; but they walked sullenly through the line of horsemen across their front. Six-shooters were discharged so close to the leaders' faces as to singe their hair, yet, under a noonday sun, they disregarded this and every other device to turn them, and passed wholly out of our control.

The foreman had to let the cattle make their own way back to the nearest water; then he rounded them up again later, and found another way across the hot and dusty plains.

In 1866, some Texas cattle were driven to Sedalia, where there was a railway from which the cattle could be shipped to the towns. Better arrangements, however, were made at Abilene; between 1867 and 1871 something like 1,460,000 cattle were driven there.

This map also shows the Western and the Pecos Trails; these were used as ranchers began to object to the long drives. In the late 1860s, thousands of miles of prairie

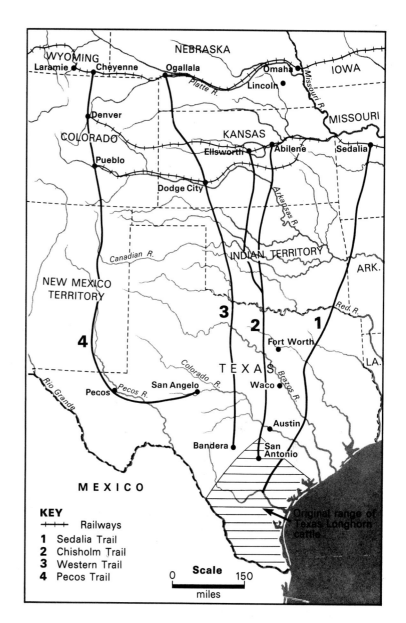

Cattle trails from Texas

were unfenced. A man owned the cattle which ordinarily grazed near water on land he claimed. Every so often, the cattle were rounded up and had a mark or 'brand' put on their skins, which other owners recognized. Nobody fed the cattle; they looked after themselves.

As the years passed, some ranchers began to improve their herds, by better feeding and breeding. They didn't want wild Texas cattle, even branded ones, driven over their land, eating their grass, drinking their water and possibly giving diseases to their better stock. So the trails had to go further and further west.

After 1874, barbed wire began to be used to fence the plains. The cowboys were enraged to see their open range fenced; and they cut the wire whenever they could. They made up a bitter song:

They say that heaven is a free range land,
Goodbye, goodbye, O fare you well;
But it's barbed wire for the devil's hat band;
And barbed wire blankets down in hell.

Farmers began crowding on to the plains. The barbed wire spread faster than it could be cut. The days of the long drive were over. Andy Adams, who made his first trip in 1882, was among the last of the cowboys on the long drive; and he took those animals to Montana, where they were to be used by the government to feed Indians. Cowboys went on working with cattle, but they no longer 'pointed 'em North'.

A cowboy's life was never easy. It was no wonder that a foreman said to James Cook when he asked for his first job:

They tell me that you can catch a cow and shoot a rabbit's eye out every pop. Now, if you can ride for the next four months without a whole night's sleep, and will turn your gun loose on any damned Indian that tries to get our horses, why, git ready. We will roll out tomorrow.

What dangers did a cowboy face in his work?

Why did the long drive end?

If the herd moved 15 or 20 miles a day, roughly how long would it take to get along the Chisholm Trail?

How different was the real cowboy's life from Hollywood and television versions of it? Why do you think the life of the 'open range' has been made to seem so wonderful?

Do you think the cowboys contributed anything permanent to the settlement of the U.S.?

11 The Union Pacific Railway

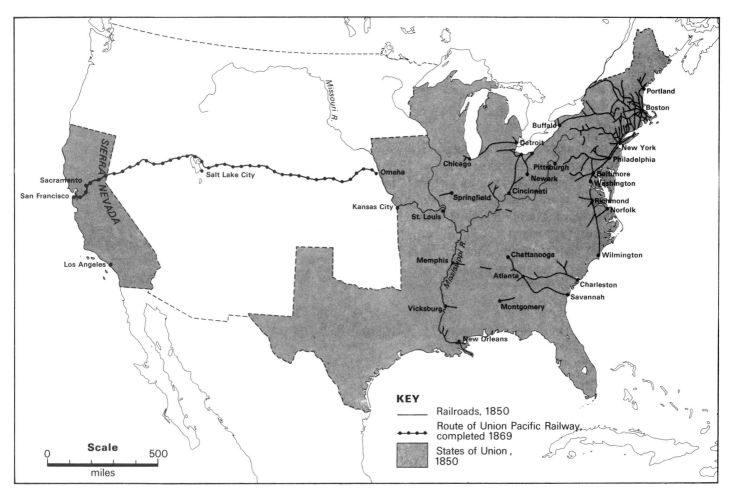

KEY

— Railroads, 1850

•—•—• Route of Union Pacific Railway, completed 1869

▨ States of Union, 1850

Scale

0 ——— 500

miles

The map shows the chief railroads existing in 1850 and the route of the Transcontinental railway. Many more railroads were built between 1850 and 1869.

Can you suggest why U.S. statesmen felt that a railway stretching right across the American continent was necessary?

(N.B. Americans often call a railway a 'railroad'; and a railway carriage, a 'railroad car'.)

Planning the route

In the middle of the nineteenth century people began to think seriously of building a railway which would cross the whole continent. Until then travellers to the far west had to go along wagon trails like the Oregon Trail (see Chapter 7) or by sea (see Chapter 13). The difficulties of building a transcontinental railway were immense. One man, who put his own money into the scheme, wrote later:

To undertake the construction of a railroad, at any price in a desert and unexplored country, its line crossing three mountain ranges at the highest elevations yet attempted on this continent, through a country swarming with hostile Indians upon a route destitute of water, except as supplied by water trains, hauled from 100 to 150 miles to thousands of men and animals engaged in construction I admit might well be regarded as the freak of a madman.

It was very difficult to decide where the railway should go, particularly as a good deal of what is now the U.S.A. had not been properly explored. To build such a railway would cost a vast amount of money; who would provide it? The railway might never be finished; and then those who had invested their money would lose it all. However, President Lincoln and other statesmen were convinced that the railway was necessary; and in 1862 the President signed an Act for the construction of a 'continuous railroad and telegraph line'. The Federal government promised to give blocks of land either side of the line, and a cash grant for each line of track laid.

Two companies were formed; they were to start building from opposite ends of the line. The Union Pacific began from the East, from Omaha; the Central Pacific from the West, at Sacramento. Much more money than the Federal government would give was needed, so both companies began to look for investors, as well as starting to build the line. Work went very slowly, at first.

The surveyors were followed, miles and miles behind, by men who flattened out or 'graded' the track. Before the lines themselves could be laid, bridges had to be built, and tunnels cut through the mountains. All the supplies needed had to be hauled along in wagons.

Building the track

General Dodge was in charge of building the Union Pacific from 1866. Afterwards he wrote:

in the mountains we sometimes had to open our grading several hundred miles ahead of our track in order to complete the grading by the time the track should reach it. All the supplies for this work had to be hauled from the end of the track, and the wagon transportation was enormous. At one time we were using at least 10,000 animals, and most of the time from 8,000 to 10,000 laborers. The bridge gangs always worked from five to twenty miles ahead of the track, and it was seldom that the track waited for a bridge. To supply one mile of track with material and supplies required about forty cars, as on the plains everything—rails, ties [sleepers], bridging, fastenings, all railway supplies, fuel for locomotives and trains, and supplies for men and animals on the entire work had to be transported from the Missouri River.

As the railway was built, bases were established, usually one or two hundred miles apart, where materials were stored, which were needed further ahead. Towns sprang

**Building the
Union Pacific
Railway in
Nebraska**

Union Pacific Railroad

up around these bases; and they were generally lawless. General Dodge wrote:

There was no law in the country, and no court. We laid out the towns, officered them, kept peace.

But one town, Julesberg, was particularly rough. Dodge sent orders that it was to be cleaned up. Later, he wrote:

When I returned to Julesberg, I asked General Casement what he had done. He replied, 'I will show you'. He took me up to a little rise just beyond Julesberg and showed me a small graveyard, saying, 'General, they all died in their boots but brought peace.'

The Plains Indians (see Chapter 8) were another problem. They needed the buffalo for food and clothing; and they saw white men shooting them and leaving the carcasses to rot on the plains, or taking away only a small part of each animal. The Indians feared that the railway would bring more white people; and they wanted to roam the plains freely as they always had. So they attacked the railway builders whenever they thought it was safe to do so, and stampeded their horses, and drove away their cattle. Dodge wrote:

Our Indian troubles commenced in 1864 and lasted until the tracks joined at Promontory. We lost most of our men and stock while building from Fort Kearney to Bitter Creek. At that time every mile of road had to be surveyed, graded, tied and bridged under military protection. The order to every surveying corps, grading, bridging and tie outfit was never to run when attacked. All were required to be armed.

THE UNION PACIFIC RAILWAY | 83

The Central Pacific had its difficulties too. The railway there had to cross the steep Sierra Nevada mountains; labour was scarce because people were hunting for gold (see Chapter 7). So immigrants from China worked on the railway. They were often supervised by Irishmen, and at first the Irishmen generally set off the gunpowder charges used to blast out the tunnels. (Later, the Chinese did it themselves.) The rock was very hard, and accidents often happened. The men made up work songs like this one:

Last week a premature blast went off,
And a mile in the sky went Big Jim Goff.
Now when next payday come around,
Jim Goff a dollar short was found.
He asked the reason; came this reply,
'You were docked for the time you were
up in the sky!'

Because they were getting money from the Federal government each company tried to race the other. Central Pacific workmen went on during the winter; an engineer wrote:

In many cases the road between camp and work was through snow tunnels, some of them 200 feet long. The construction of the retaining work in the canyons was carried on through the winter. A great dome was excavated in the snow, where the wall was to be built, and the wall stones were lowered through the shaft in the snow to the men working inside the dome. There were many snowslides. In some cases entire camps were carried away and the bodies of the men not found until the following spring.

Digging out a train after a snowstorm

Finance

The building of the railway became more and more expensive; both the Union and Central Pacific Companies needed more money than the Federal government provided. To encourage people to lend money, both railway companies arranged special trips for their shareholders and other people, along the bits of railway already built. A journalist, Richardson, wrote about one such trip, to the Donner Lake. He noticed the Chinese:

shovelling, wheeling, carting, drilling and blasting rocks and earth, while their dull, moony eyes stared out from under immense basket hats, like umbrellas.

The party stayed overnight at a small lodge, and Richardson described the scene:

The carpet was covered with maps, profiles, and diagrams, held down at the edges with candlesticks

Laying the track for the Central Pacific

Union Pacific Railroad

to keep them from rolling up. On their knees were the president, directors and surveyors, creeping from one map to another, and earnestly discussing their magnificent enterprise. The ladies of our excursion were grouped around them silent and intent, assuming liveliest interest in the dry details about tunnels, grades, excavations, 'making height' and 'getting down'. Outside the night wind moaned and shrieked, as if the Mountain Spirit resented this invasion of his ancient domain.

In spite of the difficulties the work began to go faster, especially after the end of the Civil War. No one was quite sure where the two railways would meet; and each was trying to race the other for Federal funds. There was an air of excitement about the whole thing. Someone who watched the men doing the work, W. A. Bell, wrote:

A light car, drawn by a single horse, gallops up to the front with its load of rails. Two men seize the end of a rail and start forward, the rest of the gang taking hold by twos, until it is clear of the car. They came forward at a run. At the word of command the rail is dropped in its place, right side up with care, while the same process goes on at the other side of the car. Less than thirty seconds to a rail for each gang, and so four rails go down to the minute. The moment the car is empty it is tipped over on the side of the track to let the next loaded car pass it, and then it is tipped back again, and it is a sight to see it go flying back for another load, propelled by a horse at full gallop at the end of sixty or eighty feet of rope. Close behind the first gang come the guagers, spikers and bolters, and a lively time they make of it.

The lines meet

As the two lines got nearer, the excitement mounted; each group of track levellers, the graders, was urged on. So frantic was the race, that the two groups actually passed each other. As Dodge wrote:

The laborers upon the Central Pacific were Chinamen, while ours were Irishmen, and there was much ill-feeling between them. Our Irishmen were in the habit of firing off their blasts in the cuts without giving warning to the Chinamen on the Central Pacific working right above them. From this cause several Chinamen were severely hurt. One day the Chinamen, appreciating the situation, put in what is called a 'grave' on their work, and when the Irishmen right under them were all at work let go their blast and buried several of our men. This brought about a truce at once. From that time the Irish laborers showed due respect for the Chinamen, and there was no further trouble.

Clearly, it was time to decide where the tracks should meet; eventually agreement was reached. In May, 1869, the lines were put together. (Each company had laid just one pair of lines. Trains had to pass at places where extra portions of track had been laid.) Dodge wrote:

The engineers ran up their locomotives until they touched, the engineer upon each engine breaking a bottle of champagne upon the other one, and thus the two roads were wedded into one great trunk line from the Atlantic to the Pacific.

The engines 'facing on a single track, half a world behind each back!

Union Pacific poster announcing the opening of the Transcontinental rail service.

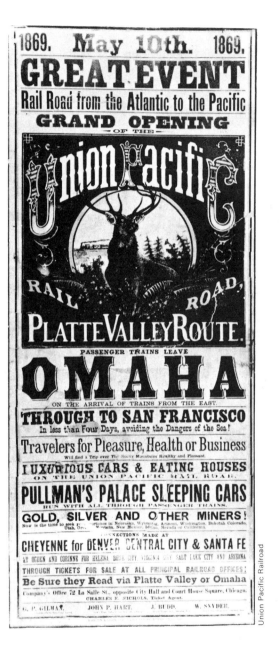

The effect of the railway

Samuel Bowles, an American who described his whole journey from Omaha to San Francisco Bay in 1869, wrote:

There will speedily be other railroads across our continent. The rivalries of sections, the temptations of commerce, the necessities of our political system, will add at least two more through lines within a generation's time. But this, the first, will forever remain the one of history; the one of romance. Its construction in so short a time was the greatest triumph of modern civilisation, of all civilisation, indeed.

Robert Louis Stevenson was one of the people who travelled from one side of the U.S. to the other. Of the journey he made in 1879, he wrote:

when day came, it was to shine upon the same broken and unsightly quarter of the world. Mile upon mile, and not a tree, a bird, or a river. Only down the long, sterile canyons the train shot hooting and awoke the resting echo. That train was the one piece of life in all the deadly land; it was the one actor, the one spectacle fit to be observed in this paralysis of man and nature. And when I think how the railroad has been pushed through this unwatered wilderness, how pigtailed Chinese pirates worked side by side with border ruffians and broken men from Europe . . . how the plumed hereditary lord of all America heard, in this last fastness, the scream of the 'bad medicine wagon' charioting his foes; and then when I go on to remember that all this epical turmoil was conducted by gentlemen in frock coats it seems to me as if this railway were the one typical achievement of the age in which we live, as if it brought together into one plot all the ends of the world and all the degrees of social rank.

What particular difficulties did the builders of the Central Pacific face?

What planning had to be done as the railway was built?

You are a newspaper reporter sent to the opening on May 10th. Describe the scene.

What struck Robert Louis Stevenson about the Union Pacific? Do you agree with him?

12 New tools for frontiersmen

Beaver traps

For many years, Indians on the Northwest coast had hunted beaver. In the 1790s, however, they began to use spring-powered traps, which they got from white men. These traps were very good; but at least one Indian saw that they might lead to disaster. Talking to an explorer, David Thompson, he said:

We are now killing the Beaver without any labor, we are now rich, but shall soon be poor, for when the Beaver are destroyed we have nothing to depend on to purchase what we want for our families, strangers now over run our country with their iron traps and we, and they will soon be poor.

The British trappers trapped in what is now Canada; the mountain men (see Chapter 6) used their iron traps all over the Rocky Mountain area. Soon beaver were harder and harder to find. The Indian's prophecy was correct.

What disadvantages did this Indian see, in the use of good iron traps?

The cotton gin

Another tool which brought with it both riches and difficulties, was invented by Eli Whitney. In 1793, this Yankee was travelling in the South, looking for a teaching job. He knew that cotton grew easily in the Southern States, but that it took a great deal of labour to get all the seeds out of it, so although it fetched a good price, it was not very profitable. Eli Whitney:

. . . heard much said of the extreme difficulty of ginning cotton; that is, of separating it from its seeds. I happened to be thinking on the subject and struck out a plan of a machine in my mind. In about ten days I made a little model. I made [a machine] which required the labor of one man to turn it and with which one man will clean ten times as much cotton as he can in any other way before known and also cleanse it much better than in the usual mode. This machine may be turned by water or with a horse, with the greatest ease, and one man and a horse will do more than fifty men with the old machines.

An early cotton gin   Science Museum

Now that cotton could be cleaned cheaply, it became a crop which planters were eager to grow. Slaves could be used to cultivate the plants, pick the cotton and clean it.

Planters looked around for land on which to grow cotton; the Indians were forced out of Georgia, Alabama, Mississippi and Florida, and planters moved in (see Chapter 3). Slaves were taken with their masters, and bought or sold willy-nilly; unless they managed to escape, as this song suggests. ('Link o' day' means day break; 'kentry' is country.)

Massa bin an' sol' yeh, O!
To go up in de kentry,
'Fo' de link o' day.
Chorus:
Run yeh! Run yeh!
'Fo' de link o' day.
Run yeh! Run yeh!
'Fo' de link o' day.

Get yeh far away, O!
An' leave yo' massa far behin'
'Fo' de link o' day.
Chorus

Dere will come a time, O!
When we will all be free,
We will all be free.
Chorus.

The slaves were not all freed until the end of the war between the Northern and Southern States in 1865.

> Do you think Whitney had any responsibility for the way in which slave owners used his machine?

The revolver

The great plains were difficult to farm because they were dry and treeless (see Chapter 9). They were hard to cross as well, because the Indians were hostile. Until Colt invented the revolver, men had to be careful not to shoot too soon, because they only had one shot before they had to stop and reload; this could mean they were killed before they could do it. In the 1840s, with Colt's 'sixshooter', the Texas Rangers found themselves superior to the Indians. After one fight, an old Indian said:

Never was a band of Indians more surprised than at this charge. They expected the Rangers to remain on the defensive, and to finally wear them out and exhaust their ammunition. In vain the Comanches tried to turn their horses and make a stand, but such was the wild confusion of running horses, popping pistols, and yelling Rangers that they abandoned the idea of a rally and sought safety in flight.

In 1850 Major Howard wrote of these revolvers:

They are the only weapon which enabled the experienced frontiersmen to defeat the *mounted* Indian. Your sixshooter is the arm which has

Messenger on the plains using a Colt revolver

rendered the name of Texas Rangers a check and terror to the bands of our frontier Indians.

What did Colt's revolver enable the white men to do?

What do you think probably happened when the Indians got hold of revolvers too? How would you find out whether you have reached the right conclusion?

Windmills

One of the greatest problems of farming or stockraising in the west was the lack of water. Streams dried up altogether in the summer, leaving the land brown and dusty. When the Union Pacific railway was built (see Chapter 11) huge windmills were made to pump up the water the engines needed. Other railways also used windmills; so did cattlemen. The farmers, however, were the people whose livelihood depended on having a windmill. Writing in 1899, Professor Barbour of the University of Nebraska noted:

What a contrast may be presented by two farms — one with cattle crowding around the well, waiting for some thoughtless farm hand to pump them their scanty allowance of water, the other where the cattle are grazing and the tanks and troughs are full and running over.

The sight of a sod house [a house made from sods of earth cut from the prairie] with flower beds and a lawn sprinkler is unexpected and almost incongruous. One would never expect to find in a ranch house marble basins and porcelain tubs. Such things exist, and are due wholly to the agency of the wind utilized by the windmill. The barest and bleakest spot is often the site chosen for the district school, but a windmill will change this barren scene in five years.

A Union Pacific engine taking in water pumped by a windmill

McCORMICK'S
PATENT
VIRGINIA REAPER.

The above cut represents one of M'Cormick's PATENT VIRGINIA REAPERS, as built for the harvest of 1846. It has been greatly improved since that time, by the addition of a seat for the driver; by a change in the position of the crank, so as to effect a direct connection between it and the sickle, (thereby very much lessening the friction and wear of the machinery, by dispensing altogether with the lever and its fixtures;) by board ribs on the reel, (which operates more gently on the grain than the round ones;) by a sheet of zinc on the platform, (which very much lessens the labor of raking;) by an increase of the size, weight and strength of the wheels of the machine, and by improvement made on the cutting apparatus.

D. W. BROWN,
OF ASHLAND, OHIO,

Having been duly appointed Agent for the sale of the above valuable labor-saving machine (manufactured by C. H. McCormick & Co., in Chicago, Ill.,) for the Counties of Seneca, Sandusky, Erie, Huron, Richland, Ashland and Wayne, would respectfully inform the farmers of those counties, that he is prepared to furnish them with the above Reapers on very liberal terms.

The Wheat portions of the above territory will be visited, and the Agent will be ready to give any information relative to said Reaper, by addressing him at Ashland, Ashland County, Ohio.

Ashland, March, 1850.

International Harvester Co.

The reaper

Farming machinery was invented in the eastern U.S.; but mechanical reapers were not much use in land littered with old tree stumps. When, however, farmers reached the open country of the plains, reapers like the one advertised here, and other machinery, were in great demand. Previously, farmers had sown only about $7\frac{1}{2}$ acres each; it was all a man could manage by himself. By 1890, however, a single farmer could cultivate 135 acres; and do a lot of the work sitting on a machine. A writer described a reaper in action, in 1880:

There is a sound of wheels. The grain disappears in an instant, then reappears; iron arms clasp it, hold it, wind it with wire, then toss it disdainfully at your feet. You hear in the rattling of the wheels the mechanism saying to itself, 'See how easy I can do it'.

> What impressed the writer of this extract? Why was he so impressed?

Barbed wire

One of the problems facing the prairie farmers was that there were few trees for fences. In 1874, Glidden took out a patent for barbed wire; this form of fencing soon spread across the prairies. The first wire was made on a very small scale, as Andrew Johnson makes clear:

I was employed as a farm hand by Joseph Glidden for about three years, and during this time he invented and began to make barb wire. In the evening, in the kitchen of his house, I would make the barbs or brads; these were made on an old-fashioned coffee mill which had been changed for this work by a blacksmith. For twisting the cable, we took the crank from an old grindstone; at this time we were working in the barn, and would make about forty feet of barb wire at a time.

Although the farmers welcomed barbed wire, not everyone else on the prairies was as enthusiastic. Cowboys, afraid that the open range was in danger, set about cutting fences wherever they could.

They say that heaven is a free range land,
Goodbye, goodbye, O fare you well;
But it's barbed wire for the devil's hat band;
And barbed wire blankets down in hell.

The stockmen, who bred cattle, were not happy either. A cowboy wrote:

The first thing that especially aroused the indignation of the stockmen was the terrible destruction to stock caused from being torn on the wire. When the first fences were made, the cattle, never having had experience with it, would run full tilt right into it, and many of them got badly hurt. After the first three years of wire fences, I have seen horses and cattle that you could hardly drive between two posts, and if there was a line of posts running across the prairie, I have seen a bunch of range horses follow the line out to the end and then turn.

The same writer, however, foresaw that barbed wire would be widely used. He wrote:

I was as confident then as I am today that wire would win and that between barbed wire and the railroads the cowboys' days were numbered.

> What were the effects of using barbed wire on the plains?

Wind Mill Power as applied for Elevators.

Eclipse Geared Mill for Power Purposes.

Stock Farm Pumping Mill.

What use were these windmills to the people who owned them?

Which of these inventions would you like to have thought of yourself? Why?

It is often said that 'necessity is the mother of invention'. From what you have read here, do you think this is true? Give reasons for your answer.

Barbed wire destroyed the open range; but it made stockbreeding and farming there profitable. Do you think inventions should ever be controlled; and if so, how and by whom?

Did any of these inventions do more harm than good?

13 Communications beyond the Mississippi

Until the first transcontinental railway was completed in 1869 (see Chapter 11) travel from one side of the U.S. to the other was a tedious and often hazardous business. Writing in 1852, a pioneer living in California advised a friend living in Germany:

The journey via the Isthmus of Panama or via San Juan de Nicaragua by steamer would not only cost a lot for a large family, but the long stay in Panama is very expensive, and one also risks catching Panama fever. It would therefore be best to make the journey from Boston or New York in a clipper ship round Cape Horn. This sort of sailing ship is very big, sails remarkably fast, and makes the journey in 90 or 100 days from New York or Boston to San Francisco. You are much more comfortable on these ships and much less exposed to danger than on the steamships. An Emigration [a party of pioneers travelling on foot] will be coming here overland this summer and autumn which it is reckoned will be at least 75,000 strong. The journey would be too troublesome for you, as it needs waggons and cattle and the necessary supplies of food have to be transported, while it requires at least 5 or 6 months for the journey from Missouri to here.

How were the Germans advised to get to California? Why?

This map shows the alternative routes suggested in the letter.

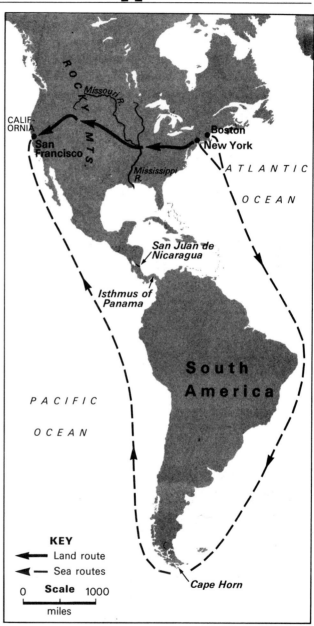

Stagecoaches

Mail and goods had to be taken across the States, as well as people. In 1858, the first stagecoach service started between the Missouri and California. The coaches, operated by the Butterfield Overland Mail Company, ran twice a week, taking 25 days for the trip.

A correspondent of the *New York Herald*, Waterman Ormsby, described the first trip:

Our road led immediately on the brink of many a precipice, over which a balky horse or a broken axle or an inexperienced driver might send us whirling in the air in a moment. There are also many abrupt curves in the road.

Most drivers would have been content to drive slowly over this spot—a distance of twelve miles and every foot of it requiring the most skillful management of the team to prevent the certain destruction of all in the coach. But our Jehu was in a hurry with the 'first States' mail' and he was bound to put us through in good time.

I held on tight as we dashed along—up and down, around the curves, and in straight lines, all at the same railroad speed. The loosening of a nut, the

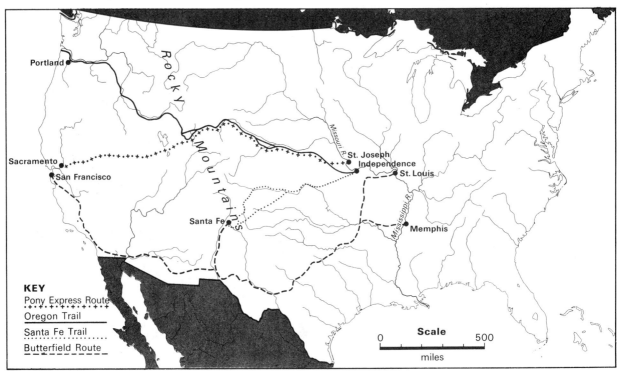

The map shows the route of the Butterfield stagecoaches, the Pony Express, and two other trails to the west.

breaking of a strap, the shying of one of the four spirited horses, might—indeed would—have sent us all to 'kingdom come'. But crack went the whip and way we flew, at a rate which I know would have made old John Butterfield, the president of the mail company, and a very experienced stage man, wish himself safely at home.

We ran the twelve miles in an hour and five minutes, and, considering the ups and downs, I thought it pretty good travelling. The mountain is covered with stunted oak trees. On the east side I noticed very few rocks. On the west this was made up by huge rusty looking crags, towering high in air.

The road over the mountain is excellent for the place and is much improved by Mr. Firebaugh, who appears to be the enterprising man of the region. He has a toll gate at the base of the mountain, charging two dollars for the passage of a single four horse team, which is cheerfully paid in consideration of what he does to the road.

The next twenty miles, to Gilroy, we travelled in two hours, and took supper. The villagers gathered around, asking all sorts of questions. 'Have plenty to eat?' 'What, beans and jerked [dried] beef?' 'Meet any Injuns?' 'None at all, eh?' 'Well that's some comfort'.

Indians attacking a Wells Fargo stagecoach

The pony express

Fast though the mails travelled by coach, William Russell thought of a faster way. In 1860, he bought 500 horses, and set up 190 way stations between St. Joseph Missouri, and San Francisco. The Pony Express riders raced in relays from station to station, and took mail from one end of the route to the other in 10 days. Mark Twain, travelling to the West, watched a rider flash by, and wrote:

The pony rider was usually a little bit of a man, brimful of spirit and endurance. No matter what time of day or night his watch came on, and no matter whether it was winter or summer, raining, snowing, hailing, or sleeting, or whether his 'beat' was a level straight road or a crazy trail over mountain crags and precipices, or whether it led through peaceful regions or regions that swarmed with hostile Indians, he must be always ready to leap into the saddle and be off like the wind! He rode fifty miles without stopping, by daylight, moonlight, starlight, or through the blackness of darkness — just as it happened. He rode a splendid horse, kept him at his utmost speed for ten miles, and then, as he came crashing up to the station where stood two men holding fast a fresh, impatient steed, the transfer of rider and mailbag was made in the twinkling of an eye, and away flew the eager pair and were out of sight before the spectator could get hardly the ghost of a look.

The life of the Pony Express was brief. In 1861, the telegraph line across the States was completed; the Pony Express went out of business.

This picture,
painted by W. H.
Jackson, shows
Western Union
workers putting up
telegraph poles as a
Pony Express rider
gallops by.

United States Information Service

Bull-trains

Heavy freight was transported either by steamboat, by rail, or by muletrains or 'bull-trains', heavy wagons hauled by teams of bulls. The 'bull-whacker' walked beside his team and controlled it by a whip. This had an 18–20 foot lash on it, the popper on the end of which the 'bull-whacker' could place within an inch of where he wanted it.

A journalist, writing in 1918, recalled bull-trains pulling into Miles City, Montana.

There were old fellows in those trains who had never done anything else but 'whack bulls' all their lives. They had started in when the Union Pacific was building across the continent just after the war, freighting to points beyond, and when the railroad

A bull-train in Miles City in 1880.

Coffrin's Old West Gallery, USA

took their job away they found it again freighting from rail points into the north, but finally the railroads had beaten them back into this strip of 'No Man's Land' in the Yellowstone valley; that the Indians had held supreme control of until a year or two before. Here the faded glory of the 'bull-train' was for a time restored. The 'mule-skinner' rode a 'wheeler' and guided his team with a jerk line. Any loafer could do that, but it took an artist to pilot a string of bulls along a side-hill road with a top-heavy load and the trail wagon pulling dead against you.

In 1895, this same journalist wrote:

The advent of the iron horse sounded the knell of the freighter and he went, no one knows whither.

Clearing the track of buffalo, 1871

Change in travel

Within a man's lifetime, transport in the Western U.S. changed beyond all recognition. Monaghan wrote in 1947, of Ezra Meeker:

Out in the State of Washington a seventy-six-year-old man with long white hair and beard started east with an ox-team along the road he had traveled westward in 1852. In 1916—aged eighty-six—he made the trip again in an automobile with a covered wagon top and a camp outfit. The daring experiment of crossing the continent in a motor car, he said, was one of his ambitions in life. And it was an achievement, people still wrote books about motoring from coast to coast. The dusty, rutted roads bore no resemblance to the modern highways tourists travel today.

The Covered Wagon proved one of the most popular pictures of the silent screen, and with its success the Overland Trail became an American epic. The year following the picture's opening an aviation meet was held. An old biplane appeared in the western sky. Two goggled figures sat in the tandem cockpit. They pulled off their helmets, and the crowd beheld white-haired Ezra Meeker, aged ninety-four. He had made his last trip, high in the air, above the Oregon Trail.

What were the hazards of riding with the Butterfield Overland Mail Company?

U.S. Post Office employees used to wear a Pony Express symbol on their uniforms. Can you suggest why a service lasting for so short a time should have been so long remembered?

What were a bull-whacker's skills? Why did he become redundant?

None of these extracts refers solely to railways. Using the extracts, however, explain why the building of railways in the west would make a difference to people's lives.

What industries, do you think, must have grown and died as transport methods changed in the west?